W9-AOX-684

BASEBALL
SUPERSTARS

Kirby Puckett

Hank Aaron

Ty Cobb

Lou Gehrig

Derek Jeter

Randy Johnson

Mike Piazza

Kirby Puckett

Jackie Robinson

Ichiro Suzuki

Bernie Williams

✫ ✫ ✫ ✫ ✫ ✫ ✫ ✫ ✫ ✫ ✫ ✫ ✫ ✫ ✫ ✫

BASEBALL SUPERSTARS

Kirby Puckett

Rachel A. Koestler-Grack

✫ ✫ ✫ ✫ ✫ ✫ ✫ ✫ ✫ ✫ ✫ ✫ ✫ ✫ ✫ ✫

KIRBY PUCKETT

For information, contact:

Chelsea House
An imprint of Infobase Publishing
132 West 31st Street
New York NY 10001

Library of Congress Cataloging-in-Publication Data
Koestler-Grack, Rachel A., 1973-
Kirby Puckett / Rachel A. Koestler-Grack.
p. cm. — (Baseball superstars)
Includes bibliographical references and index.
ISBN-13: 978-0-7910-9497-6
ISBN-10: 0-7910-9497-9
1. Puckett, Kirby—Juvenile literature. 2. Baseball players—United States—Biography—Juvenile literature. I. Title. II. Series.
GV865.P83K64 2007
796.357092—dc22
[B] 2007006207

Chelsea House books are available at special discounts when purchased in bulk quantities for businesses, associations, institutions, or sales promotions. Please call our Special Sales Department in New York at (212) 967-8800 or (800) 322-8755.

You can find Chelsea House on the World Wide Web at http://www.chelseahouse.com

Series design by Erik Lindstrom
Cover design by Ben Peterson

Printed in the United States of America

Bang EJB 10 9 8 7 6 5 4 3 2 1

This book is printed on acid-free paper.

All links and Web addresses were checked and verified to be correct at the time of publication. Because of the dynamic nature of the Web, some addresses and links may have changed since publication and may no longer be valid.

CONTENTS

The Catch

On October 26, 1991, the fans at the Metrodome in Minneapolis, Minnesota, fidgeted in their seats. It was Game 6 of the World Series, and Minnesota was trailing the Atlanta Braves, three games to two. The Twins needed to win this game to tie the series and go to a final seventh game. In the third inning, that prospect looked promising. The Twins were leading, 2-0, and the Braves were up to bat. Atlanta's Terry Pendleton waited on first base as Ron Gant stepped up to the plate. Gant swung hard on an inside pitch and caught it right on the meat of the barrel. *Crack!*

After more than 500 games at the Metrodome, center fielder Kirby Puckett knew almost instinctively when a ball was going back to the warning track, the outfield wall, barely over the wall, or way over the wall. On this hit, his first

reaction was, "Uh-oh! That may be outta here." As he raced toward the wall in left-center with his eyes on the ball, he realized the hit was not going out of the park. He could catch

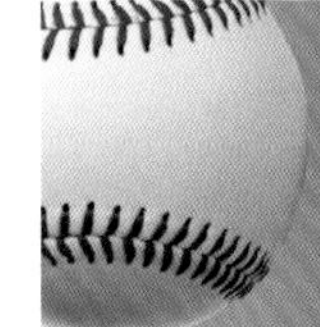

☆☆☆☆☆☆

IN THEIR OWN WORDS

"In 1991 in playing against him in the World Series, if we had to lose and if one person basically was the reason, you never want to lose but you didn't mind it being [to] Kirby Puckett. When he made the catch and when he hit the home run, you could tell the whole thing had turned. His name just seemed to be synonymous with being a superstar."

—Atlanta Braves pitcher John Smoltz

"Kirby played the game with such passion and enthusiasm that he was beloved by players and fans throughout all of baseball. An icon in Minnesota, Kirby's contributions to the game and all who love it will stand as a lasting tribute to his life."

—Donald M. Fehr, executive director of the Major League Baseball Players Association

"The clubhouse was alive when he walked in. I shouldn't say walk in, because he was there before everybody else. It was just amazing. That Game 6 [of the 1991 World Series]—every day he would put his whole team on his back: 'Hop on, boys.' That was his favorite line—hop on. 'Puck will take care of you.'

That's the way you play baseball—the way he hustled, the way he ran. Just having fun. You didn't know if he was 0-for-25 or 25-for-27, you didn't know. He was the same every single day. You need a model in baseball to follow, and I tried to figure out how he did it every day. I tried, but he did it."

—Jacque Jones, former Twin now with Cubs

this ball. At the wall, he took a huge leap into the air and caught the ball against the plexiglass window pane above the padded fence line. He had stolen Gant's home run like only Kirby Puckett could do. After the catch, Gant kicked the dirt in disgust.

Puckett, though, had not seen Gant's reaction because he was wheeling to throw back to first. With a nearly "shoo-in" home run, Puckett figured that Pendleton was way off the first-base bag. In fact, so sure the hit was going to be a bomb, Pendleton had already rounded second base. He scurried to get back to first base. Puckett's throw was on target but just barely missed getting Pendleton out. Still, in the stands, the spectators went wild.

Among Twins fans, Puckett's play later became known as "The Catch." Plenty of game was left to go, however. In the fifth inning, Pendleton hit a two-run homer to tie the game. The Twins also scored a run in the fifth inning, once again putting them in the lead. Then, in the seventh inning, the Braves scored another run to tie the game again. The game stretched into extra innings.

In the eleventh inning, Puckett and teammate Al Newman noticed Braves pitcher Charlie Leibrandt getting up in the bullpen. Atlanta was changing pitchers. Immediately, Puckett and Newman had a flashback to the 1987 race against the Kansas City Royals to win the American League West. At that time, Leibrandt was pitching for Kansas City. He started the game in which Minnesota clinched a tie for the division. In that game, Newman began a rally with a double, and the Twins followed with three home runs—Puckett to the blue seats in right center, Gary Gaetti to left field, and Kent Hrbek to right field.

"I can hit [off] this guy!" Puckett thought to himself, when he saw Leibrandt warming up.

When Leibrandt trotted to the mound to start the inning, Newman said, "Puck, here comes your man."

A jubilant Kirby Puckett rounded the bases after hitting the winning home run in the eleventh inning of Game 6 of the World Series in 1991. Earlier in the game, he made a spectacular catch to rob Ron Gant of the Atlanta Braves of a home run. The victory tied the series and gave Puckett's team, the Minnesota Twins, the chance to play in Game 7.

"Yeah, he is," Puckett said flatly, trying not to be overconfident. Puckett was leading off, the first batter of the inning. Teammate Chili Davis was next. As the two of them stood on deck swinging their bats, Davis said, "Go ahead and get this over with."

"That's my plan!" Puckett responded, though he was unsure how to get it done. "What should I do here?"

"Just make this guy get the ball up," Davis answered, meaning that Puckett should wait to take the right pitch. Puckett was usually a "hack" batter who would often swing at the first pitch.

When Puckett stepped into the box, the crowd's roar was deafening. He felt his spine tingling. On the first pitch, he waited—ball one, down and away. Puckett stepped out of the box and grinned at Davis, who laughed. He took the next pitch—ball two, down and away. Then, Leibrandt threw a ball up under Puckett's chin, but the umpire called it a strike. The count was 2-and-1, a batter's count. On the fourth pitch, Puckett swung and hit a bomb to deep center—home run. The Metrodome erupted into sheer madness, with fans fiercely waving their Homer Hankies. Even Puckett jumped and screamed as he rounded the bases. The Twins were going to Game 7 of the World Series.

At five feet, eight inches (172 centimeters) and 210 pounds (95 kilograms), Kirby Puckett did not have a typical baseball build. In his early years, scouts laughed at the thought of Puckett ever becoming a great major leaguer. Puckett, though, refused to listen to them. He knew in his heart that he was born to play baseball, and he defied the odds. From the time he first stormed the major leagues in 1984 until his premature retirement in 1996, Puckett represented everything that baseball was meant to be. His smile, hustle, attitude, and charisma captured the hearts of fans throughout the country, especially in Minnesota. He earned respect and admiration from fans, coaches, teammates, and ballplayers throughout the league.

His remarkable journey from the public-housing projects in South Chicago to his all-star career with the Minnesota Twins stands as an inspiration to young people. Along the way, he never lost who he was or how he played. "[He] stayed true to himself," NBC broadcaster Bob Costas said. "And that's very rare."

Hope Is Born

Some people have called the Robert Taylor Homes in South Chicago "the place where hope dies." Down the Dan Ryan Expressway, about one mile south of Comiskey Park, 28 buildings dotted a two-mile stretch of South State Street. These apartment buildings were the Robert Taylor Homes, more commonly called the "projects." Public-housing projects are owned and operated by a government agency and are usually rented out to low-income families. The Robert Taylor Homes had a reputation as one of the worst housing projects in the country. The area was shrouded in violence, drugs, and gangs. No one expected the kids who grew up there to ever amount to anything.

On March 14, 1960, life in the projects was not much better than it is today. Hope, though, was born to William and

Catherine Puckett. His name was Kirby, the youngest of nine Puckett children. Kirby had three sisters—June, Frances, and Jacqueline—and five brothers—Charles (the oldest, at 22), William, twins Donnie and Ronnie, and Spencer. When Kirby was born, only Jackie and six-year-old Spencer were still living in the three-bedroom apartment on the 14th floor they called home. Their Robert Taylor Homes apartment building was at the corner of State and 43rd streets, address 4444 South State Street.

Growing up, Kirby did not have fancy toys, but he always had food, clothes, and lots of love. His parents provided for him as best they could. William juggled two jobs. From six in the morning until noon, he worked at a downtown department store. After having lunch and a couple of hours rest, he left again at four in the afternoon, this time for his job as a supervisor at the main post office. Kirby was in bed asleep long before his father got home late at night. The post office was closed on Saturdays and Sundays, and William only worked at the department store on Saturdays. After work on Saturdays, William picked up groceries downtown because they were cheaper there than in the small shops in the Pucketts' neighborhood. The Pucketts never owned a car when Kirby was young. In fact, neither William nor Catherine even had a driver's license. Instead, they took the bus. On Saturdays, William would call home and have Kirby meet him at the bus stop to help carry the grocery bags. Sundays, William had off. Still, Kirby rarely got to spend time with his father.

With William gone so much, raising the family mostly fell into Catherine's hands. She was the driving force in Kirby's life. Born in Charleston, Missouri, Catherine married William when she was only 15 years old. "She would hang around the cow pasture where the men would play baseball, and that's where they met," said Catherine's only sister, Salitha Smith, in Chuck Carlson's book *Kirby Puckett: Baseball's Last Warrior*. "She was a sweetheart darling who was always more concerned about others than herself." Shortly after their marriage, they moved to the projects in Chicago, where Catherine gave birth to her first child, Charles.

Knowing how much William enjoyed baseball, it was no surprise to Catherine Puckett that Kirby found a passion for it. He played baseball every minute he could, with whatever materials were handy—whether it was a balled-up piece of aluminum foil or socks rolled up tight and wrapped with tape. Like most mothers, Catherine would always tell Kirby, "Don't play in the house." But like most kids, Kirby did not always listen. His best friend would come over, and they would hit and throw the ball around. On occasion, they would break something, which was followed by a good spanking.

Then, Kirby and his buddy would take the baseball game outside. They painted a square on the wall of the building to mark off a strike zone. Those squares covered the sides of almost all the Robert Taylor buildings. Most of the boxes were way too large. For this reason, years later, Kirby's strike zone was also big. When the kids were not using aluminum foil or socks, they played with rubber balls that cost 10 or 15 cents apiece. At that time, Kirby received an allowance of $1 a week. With his money, he could buy two rubber balls and about 80 pieces of candy. "My friends lasted till the candy ran out!" he later said.

Of course, playing in a city neighborhood instead of on a ball field called for special rules. The buildings at Robert Taylor were far enough apart that, if any fly ball hit another building, it was called a home run. One bounce before the ball hit a wall was a triple, two bounces a double. The kids usually played with one pitcher and two fielders, which meant there was no such thing as a ground-ball out. They had a system depending on how many players showed up. Sometimes they had four or five boys. If more than five wanted to play, though, they would take the game to a nearby asphalt field, which was complete with painted bases. On the field, they used a hard ball instead of the

For the first 12 years of his life, Kirby Puckett grew up in the Robert Taylor Homes, a 28-building housing project that stretched for two miles on the South Side of Chicago. The public-housing complex, pictured here, had a reputation for crime, but it was also where Kirby began to learn baseball, playing makeshift games in and around the buildings.

rubber balls. Kirby was not afraid of skinned knees. He slid into those bases in his shorts.

No matter how many guys wanted to play, Kirby could always be counted on to show up. If no one else did, he entertained himself by tossing the ball up in the air and hitting it against the wall.

The tenants at Robert Taylor did not mind the boys and their games, but the janitors did. They were trying to grow grass, and the ball games tore up the lawn. Whenever the boys spotted the janitors, they had to take off running. They had to keep one eye on the ball and one eye out for the janitors at all times.

Because there was no Little League at the projects, these neighborhood games were how Kirby played baseball until he went to high school. During the summer, he would run out the door by eight in the morning, play ball all day, and head home at sunset. Often, he would not come home until he heard his mother's voice calling from the 14th floor, "Kiiiiiirrby! . . . KIRBY!" Whether he was hitting a ball against the side of their building or playing three buildings away, he could usually hear her yelling and knew it was time to head home.

Kirby had to be home when the streetlights came on. After dark, trouble started in the streets. He could stay out on the 14th-floor balcony but never on the ground. At night, gangs prowled the neighborhood. Although Robert Taylor was safer in those days than in later years, Kirby still heard gun shots on some nights. The Pucketts may have had their share of problems, but fortunately all of their children turned out well. "For nine of us children to grow up and get out of the ghetto and be good, law-abiding citizens, that's a blessing in itself," Kirby Puckett later said, in Carlson's book. Puckett attributed that to his parents. "My personal role models were my mom and dad."

Of all the kids, Kirby got into trouble the least. Catherine was determined to keep the baby of the family safe. Kirby did not hang out, and he rarely even went to the movies. At night, he stayed home. Baseball and school were his whole life.

HIGH SCHOOL DAYS

When Kirby was 12 years old and the only child still at home, his father earned a promotion at the post office. His family finally moved out of the Robert Taylor Homes and into a better apartment on 79th Street at Wolcott Avenue, also on the South Side of Chicago. There, Kirby made a few more friends, some of whom became his friends for life. Every Friday and Saturday night, the boys would get together at someone's house to eat pizza and watch basketball games on television.

Kirby did not get the chance to play any organized baseball until he went to Calumet High School at age 15. Those neighborhood games must have paid off, though, because he earned All-America honors playing third base. During high school ball, Kirby received excellent coaching from James McGhee. The coach showed him how to hit a curveball and taught him to concentrate on watching the ball all the way from the time it left the pitcher's hand. To achieve the effect of a major-league curveball, McGhee cut a slice out of a baseball so it would curve a lot in any kind of breeze.

There was never a doubt in Kirby's mind that he had what it took to be a ballplayer. The scouts, however, never came to see the team play at Calumet High. They were too scared to come to that neighborhood, and Kirby could hardly blame them. Although the neighborhood may not have been as rough as Robert Taylor, it was still considered dangerous. The school did not even have a real field, and there were no outfield fences. If a player hit a line drive through a gap, the batter just kept running. There were plenty of "inside the park" homers.

In school, Kirby was an average to above-average student. He skipped a few classes, as some high school students do, but all he did was go to the cafeteria for a snack. On one of these occasions, Kirby was skipping Mrs. Singleton's English class.

She had a reputation as a pretty nice teacher, as long as you did not cross her. Somehow, Mrs. Singleton found out that Kirby was in the cafeteria eating lunch instead of attending her class. She marched right into the cafeteria and ordered him back to class. Kirby was so embarrassed he wanted to crawl under the table. He was trying to be a cool guy and skip class, but he ended up getting caught in front of all of his friends. After that day, he never skipped class again.

During the summers, Kirby was invited to play on teams with guys who were four or five years older. One of these teams was a semipro squad with some of the best players in Chicago. Formally called the Chicago Pirates, the team was more commonly known as the Askew Pirates, named after Roosevelt Askew—a pool-hall owner who put the team together.

At this time, the Pittsburgh Pirates were wearing all different styles of uniforms—pinstripes, white, and black, and different caps, too, round, flat, and so on. The Askew Pirates also had six or seven combinations of uniforms. Kirby could play whenever he wanted. He would just call up and say, "'Kew, I want to play today," and Askew told him where the game was going to be.

Some scouts watched those semipro games. Also, they showed up for the annual South Side/North Side all-star high school game. Any scout who saw Kirby, though, probably thought he was too small to be a major-league ballplayer. Kirby knew he was shorter than most players, but his size did not stop him. Throughout his childhood, his mother always encouraged him by saying, "You can do it, Kirby." And toward the end of his high school career, Catherine started saying, "You can make the major leagues, Kirby." And Kirby believed her.

Catherine, however, did not have a positive attitude all the time. She was against football, probably because she thought it was too dangerous. Her message was simple: "You cannot play football." So Kirby never played football, other than in neighborhood games. He could, however, try out for the basketball team. One year, he took a stab at the varsity team but did not make the cut. So baseball became Kirby's number-one love.

FULL SCHOLARSHIP

By the time he graduated in 1979, Kirby Puckett thought he was good enough at baseball to play in the minor leagues, and maybe even the majors. A few other people thought so, too, and Catherine said she had no doubt that he would someday be a big-league ballplayer. Puckett later admitted, "But moms are always that way."

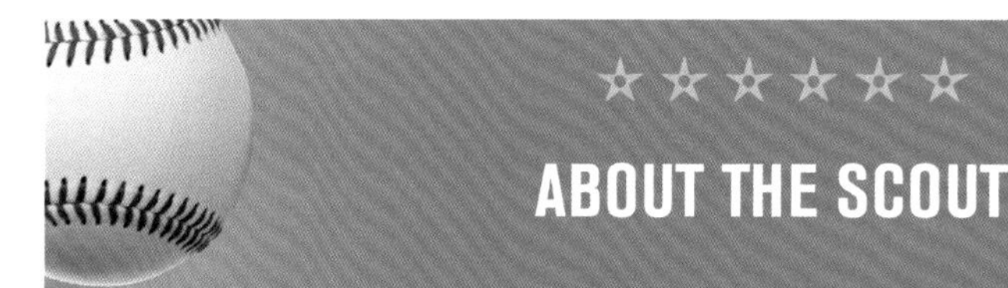

ABOUT THE SCOUT

Professional sports scouts are trained talent finders who travel from city to city to watch athletes play. For instance, baseball scouts visit various ball clubs around the country looking for good ballplayers. They evaluate each player's skill level and decide which players would be best for their team.

Some scouts follow *prospects*, or younger players who may require future training and development. Usually, the scout can tell if the athlete will develop into a strong ballplayer with the proper coaching. In these cases, the expense of the extra training is well worth the potential pay-off, especially if the player becomes an all-star. Other scouts will only focus on players who are polished and ready for the big leagues.

Many scouts are former coaches or retired players who have years of experience within a sports organization. Others have simply made a career out of being a scout. Skilled scouts who can help put together a solid team can make the difference between winning and losing, as well as affect the team's financial success or failure.

He was not totally focused on pro ball at the time, and the best college-scholarship offer he had was from a school in Miami, Florida. It was a solid junior-college program, but Miami was a long way from Chicago. Still the baby of the family, Puckett wanted to stay close to his parents. So he told them, according to his book *I Love This Game!*, "Hey, I'm 18. I'm a man, or almost a man. I don't want to go to school right now. I want to take a year to see what the real world is like."

He took a job at the Ford Motor plant on Torrence Avenue, on the South Side of Chicago. He worked on the fast-paced

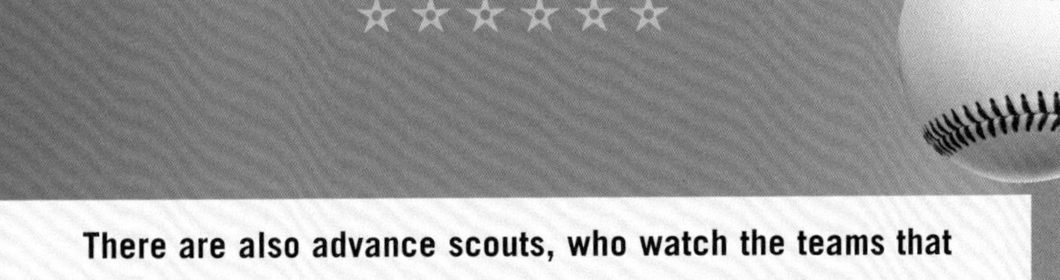

There are also advance scouts, who watch the teams that their team is going to play. As these scouts watch the game, they take notes about the opposing team's offensive and defensive strengths and weaknesses. Afterward, they develop strategies that will help their team win the game.

When scouts watched Kirby Puckett in his early years, they did not think that he had the skill to be a major-league ballplayer. Major leaguers are usually much taller than Puckett was. What they did not know yet was that Puckett could really jump. He could even dunk a basketball. He also had incredible speed. In his college days, he bragged that he could run 60 yards (55 meters) in 6.3 seconds. His coach laughed at the idea. So Puckett offered to prove it. On his first try, he ran the distance in 6.05, but the coach claimed he had jumped the gun. The next time, he ran a clean 6.3. Later, he ran the distance in 6.45 *uphill*. Puckett had power and speed that a lot of scouts failed to see.

assembly line in charge of laying the carpet in Thunderbirds. "If you own one of those vintage models," Puckett later said, "I might have installed the rug in that beauty." He stood beside a stack of rugs, already arranged in the right order to match the color of the Thunderbirds coming down the line. Later, he admitted that it was good that he did not have to worry about matching up the color, because he had little time to think. He had less than a minute to throw a rug into each car and fit it over some bolts sticking out of the floor. Down the line, the next station would then install the seats and bolt everything in.

Every morning, Puckett rode an express bus to the plant. If he missed it, he was out of a ride. So he made sure he never missed it. He earned about $8 an hour, plus some overtime. For Puckett, it seemed like a fortune. Every paycheck, he took home $500 after taxes, some of which went to help his mother and father pay bills.

At the time, Ford Motor Company policy stated that an employee would become an official union member after working at the plant for 90 days. The company let Puckett go on the eighty-ninth day. Next, he took a temporary job with the Census Bureau. When that job came to an end, Puckett knew he had to make a plan. He would either have to find a permanent job or take a college scholarship. The major-league clubs were holding summer mini-camps in Chicago. Puckett signed up for the one at McKinley Park, not far from Comiskey Park. Basically, the camp was for high school players, but anyone could sign up. If a player had talent and he did not look like a fluke, he could possibly sign a minor-league contract.

When Puckett showed up on the first day, the park was a zoo. Hundreds of guys were standing around, while the scouts and coaches running the circus divided them up among six baseball diamonds. First, they ran some drills and then picked teams for games, with Puckett playing his regular position at third base. They played all day, from 10 in the morning until dark.

Kirby Puckett runs the base path during a game between the Minnesota Twins and the Chicago White Sox at Comiskey Park, near where he grew up. Few scouts gave Puckett a good look because of his small stature—he was 5-foot-8. Dewey Kalmer, the coach of the Bradley University baseball team, though, saw that Puckett had speed and strength, and he offered Puckett a scholarship to the school.

Puckett's contact at the camp was Art Stewart, the local scout for the Kansas City Royals. At one point in the day, Stewart came over to Puckett, and they talked for a while. While they were chatting, Dewey Kalmer—the baseball coach at Bradley University in Peoria, Illinois—interrupted. "I've checked your grades, and you graduated with a B average," Kalmer said, according to *I Love This Game!* "How would you like to come to Bradley University on a full scholarship?"

Puckett could hardly believe his ears. He started to say "Yes!" but then decided that he better discuss the offer with his parents first. When he got home, he burst through the front door and shouted out the news. "Really?" they asked. "Really?" They just could not believe it, either.

It was true, though, and this time, Puckett was ready for college. Unlike the school in Miami, Bradley University was only a two-and-a-half-hour bus ride from Chicago. He would still be close enough to come home from time to time. William and Catherine told him to go back and accept the scholarship.

Later, Puckett learned that one of the main reasons the Royals—and other major-league teams that had seen him play—had not drafted him was his small stature. They could see and measure his speed, but he was not a "can't miss" prospect in their eyes, not at 155 pounds (70 kilograms). There just were not a lot of "little guys" in the big leagues. At the time, Puckett was thrilled to pick up the scholarship. He still did not see baseball as his destiny, even though he certainly would have signed a contract on the spot. "The truth is I might have signed a contract right out of high school and never made it past A-ball," Puckett later wrote in his autobiography. "Maybe I needed that year off to grow. Call me a late bloomer."

Each year there are hundreds of exceptional high school baseball players, and they all need a huge break, or even several of them, to really catch somebody's attention. Dewey Kalmer gave Puckett one of those breaks when he offered the scholarship to Bradley. It almost seemed as if fate had a hand in the whole event. Normally, college coaches are not allowed at mini-camps, because the coaches are in competition with the major-league teams for players. Luckily for Puckett, Art Stewart had invited Kalmer. That summer, Kalmer saw a player with running speed, bat speed, and an average arm. One other attribute, though, stood out above the rest—overall strength. Kalmer believes that strength is the common denominator in great athletes. Even though this runt of a baseball player could only hit a fastball, Kalmer took a chance on Kirby Puckett.

Honing His Game

In the fall of 1980, Kirby Puckett hopped on a Greyhound bus to Bradley, and Dewey Kalmer met him at the station. The dorms were crowded that year, and on the first night, Puckett's bed was a super-sized piece of foam on a dorm-room floor. This arrangement was not exactly what Puckett had in mind, especially because he was on scholarship. The next day, he told Kalmer that he was not sleeping on the floor again. So Puckett moved into some kind of bunk, jammed with a handful of other guys. Although he did not want to be rude, Puckett knew that this place was not going to work either. Once again, he went to Kalmer. This time, he told Kalmer that, if he had housing money and meal money, he could find his own place to live. Kalmer agreed, and Puckett and three other ballplayers found a duplex to rent. Only half a block from campus, the place even had a working fireplace, a first for Puckett.

Less than a month later, Puckett's father died. Kalmer gave him permission to stay at home as long as was needed. Because his other brothers and sisters were all grown and had moved away, Puckett felt it was his responsibility to step up as the new man of the house. After staying three weeks or so, Puckett told his mother, Catherine, "I don't want to go back to school, Ma. I'm going to stay home and take care of you."

"You're going back to school," Catherine shot back. "I've got too many gloves and too many bats and balls invested in you. Plus, you're something special. You're going to make it one day." So once again, Puckett packed his bag and left for Bradley, while Catherine stayed by herself in the apartment on 79th Street in Chicago.

In the beginning, baseball at Bradley was disappointing. Originally, Kalmer had told Puckett that he would play third base, just as he had wanted. When the scrimmages started that fall, though, Puckett was not playing anywhere. As it turned out, Kalmer had an infield of all seniors. It did not take Puckett long to figure out that he would be sitting on the bench a lot that season. The best he could hope for was some playing time in the late innings, mostly as a pinch runner. In that area, he did well—10 for 10 in stolen bases to help win some games. Nevertheless, this role was not enough.

Maybe Puckett should not have expected to play much that season. But in Puckett's mind, he was there to play baseball. His mother expected him to play baseball. Maybe he was out of line, but one day he finally got the nerve to talk to the coach.

"Dewey, you gave me a baseball scholarship," Puckett said, as recounted in his autobiography. "You told me I was going to play third base, and I get here, and you've already got an all-senior infield." Kalmer agreed that events had not worked out as he had planned and that he would think about the situation overnight.

The next day, Kalmer approached Puckett during practice and asked if he could play the outfield. Puckett told him, "I [can] play anywhere [you] put me. *Anywhere*." So he put Puckett in center field. By the time the spring games began (after the cold-weather layoff), Puckett was the starting center fielder. He led the team in home runs and stolen bases. He hit about .400 and drove in more than 50 runs. During one doubleheader, Puckett reached base eight or nine times, and he was sure some scouts were watching him that afternoon.

That year, Puckett made the All-Missouri Valley Conference team, but he left Bradley following that season anyway. After his three-week absence in the fall, he just could not catch up on his studies, and his grades plummeted. To be eligible next fall, he would have had to go to summer school. Puckett did not want to do that. He did not want to be so far from his mother all summer long.

When he left Bradley, he thanked Dewey Kalmer for all his help. Kalmer had helped Puckett straighten out one major problem he had back then: pulling off the ball. Kalmer threw a spare tire around Puckett's neck, resting it on the right shoulder. The tire kept Puckett's left arm and shoulder from flying out of sync. On the day Puckett walked out of Kalmer's office, Kalmer would have described him as a hungry ballplayer who badly wanted to make it but who was not that good yet. Puckett needed a lot of polishing. Still, he once told a scout that this Puckett kid would turn into a great major leaguer. The scout laughed.

INTEREST FROM THE BIG LEAGUES

The following summer, Puckett played ball in the Central Illinois Collegiate League, a summer league for college players. That was when another big break came his way. During the summer of 1981, the major-league players went on strike. A compromise over the issue in dispute could not be reached, and the ballplayers decided that the only way to force one was to walk off the field. At the time, Puckett did not follow the events too closely. The majors seemed so far into the future to him. All he knew was that he wanted the teams to start to play again. The shutdown, however, was the key to Puckett's next break. With the league frozen, Jim Rantz, a scout for the Minnesota Twins, was free to watch his son Mike play a game in Puckett's collegiate league.

Puckett played on the opposing team. All in all that day, he had a good game—he had a home run and a couple of other hits, stole a couple of bases, and threw a guy out at home. He was hitting about .400 at the time. What stood out most to Rantz, though, was that Puckett was the only player out there who was not dragging. The heat that day was incredible, and only 20 people were in the stands. Many players were less than enthusiastic about playing. Puckett was the one guy who really looked excited. "I was not only impressed by his performance on the field," Rantz said in *Kirby Puckett: Baseball's Last Warrior*, "but it was a very hot day, and Kirby was the first player on and off the field. There were 15 to 20 people in the stands after the game, [and] he came by to say hello to everybody." Little did Puckett know, but Rantz began to watch his statistics that summer. When it came time for the winter draft in January 1982, Rantz threw in Puckett's name. He was the Twins' first pick—the third in the country overall.

By this time, Puckett had enrolled at Triton College in River Grove, Illinois. Shortly after he left Bradley, he had gotten in touch with the coach at Triton—Bob Symonds. The Triton baseball program had an excellent reputation—even the ball field was impressive. Also, the school was practically right in Chicago. Puckett called Symonds, explained his situation, told him how he had done at Bradley, and Symonds welcomed him to Triton.

While Puckett was playing at Triton, Tom Hull, a representative for the Twins, approached him to negotiate a contract. Hull stopped over at Catherine's apartment a couple of times

MAJOR LEAGUE BASEBALL STRIKE

The Major League Baseball strike of 1981 was the fifth time in major-league history that play stopped. The strike, which forced the cancellation of 713 games, grew out of a dispute over free agency. In the mid-1970s, the team owners lost in arbitration over the issue of free agency, which gave players the right to sign a new contract with another team at the end of their current contract. Before then, clubs would decide whether to keep a player and make him sign a new contract with them. The player did not have a choice in the matter. Essentially, the player was the property of the team.

In 1981, the owners desperately wanted to win back exclusive rights over the players. If they could not keep a player, they wanted to be compensated for losing him to another team. The "losing" owners demanded the right to choose a player from the "winning" team's roster (excluding 12 "protected" players who could not be touched). Baseball players argued that this demand went against the whole concept of free agency. When the owners refused to budge, the players walked off the field on June 12. Although the players called the strike, most sportswriters and fans blamed the owners.

On July 31, a compromise was finally reached. In the settlement, all unprotected players from all teams were placed in a "players drawing pool." Teams that lost a star free agent could draw a player from the pool to replace their loss. In this way, the draw affected all clubs, not just the signing club. Play in the 1981 season resumed on August 10.

and took the two Pucketts out to dinner. He treated them like royalty. At first, Catherine did most of the talking. Then, Hull mentioned that there was a $2,000 bonus to sign. At once,

Another Major League Baseball strike in 1994 resulted in the cancellation of the World Series for the first time in 90 years. This time, the owners demanded a salary cap, a limit on the amount of money a team could spend on players' salaries. They claimed that, unless the teams agreed to share local broadcasting revenue and enact a salary cap, small-market teams—like the Twins—would not be able to compete. On January 18, 1994, the owners approved a new revenue-sharing plan attached to a salary cap, which needed player approval.

Naturally, the players vehemently opposed the plan. Donald Fehr, the executive director of the Major League Baseball Players Association, rejected the offer. He believed a salary cap was simply a way for the owners to clean up their own problems with no benefit to the players. The strike began on August 12, 1994, and lasted 232 days, until April 2, 1995.

The strike finally ended without a compromise; players took the field once again. This time, however, the strike left many fans disgusted. They were angry that money could cancel the World Series, when the Spanish flu, two world wars, the Great Depression, earthquakes, and other disasters could not. On Opening Day around the country, attendance was meager, and many fans were hostile toward the players. Attendance across the United States hit an all-time low, proving that fans won't always support a strike.

On the twelfth day of a strike by baseball players in 1981, the New York Yankees put up a sign at Yankee Stadium apologizing to fans. In an indirect way, the strike helped Kirby Puckett's career. The walkout gave Jim Rantz, a scout with the Minnesota Twins, time to see his son play a semipro game. Puckett was on the opposing team, and his play and stamina during the game impressed Rantz. The Twins drafted Puckett the following January.

Puckett interrupted, "Two thousand dollars! I worked for the Ford Motor Company making two thousand dollars in a month. Come on, now, really!"

At first, Puckett thought Hull was joking around with that offer, but he was serious. Hull explained that teams do not offer much money in the January draft, which was reserved for junior-college players and college dropouts. Today, the major leagues do not even have a January draft, because there are not that many players eligible. Back then, the idea was that, if a team could sign a player cheap in the winter, great. Otherwise, wait until the June draft and try again. Even after Puckett understood, he still said no to the offer.

A couple of days later, Hull called and said he wanted to try again. Hull had talked to George Brophy, the Twins' farm director, and received the go-ahead to make a better offer. This time, Hull took the Pucketts to the best steak house in Chicago. He proposed an offer of $6,000. Still, Puckett said no way. He had played very well during the summer season, and the fall season at Triton had also gone well. Scouts were always hanging around Triton, and Puckett's name was becoming more well known. Being picked third overall in the January draft only helped. Puckett felt confident that, if he had a good spring season, he would be drafted again in June—when the real money was dished out. He had no problems passing up six grand.

Hull was not about to give up. He had planned another meeting with the stubborn Puckett kid, but he had a heart attack and died before the meeting ever took place. Nevertheless, it was not just Hull who was interested in Puckett—it was the Twins. They decided to wait until after the junior-college season to pursue him. That worked out fine for Puckett. Triton turned out to be the best baseball experience he had ever had. First of all, the team was good—with a 60–10 record at the end of the year. About 10 players from the team were drafted in the first three rounds the following summer.

The practice time was invaluable. They practiced in the snow after shoveling off the field. Bob Symonds had them take infield practice from the warning track, the gravel ring surrounding the outfield. Puckett calls that "long toss," and it is one reason his arm became so strong. The team worked on bunting for hours, and the results paid off for the rest of Puckett's career. In Puckett's mind, Symonds was the most influential coach he ever had, and he helped shape Puckett into the great player he became.

Some of the scouts who had seen Puckett in the summer league thought he should be playing infield—second base maybe. They were probably worried about his size. Deep down, Puckett knew he was an outfielder, but young players listen to everybody. Puckett told Symonds what the scouts had said, so the coach tried him at second base. After a couple of weeks, Puckett wanted to be back in the outfield. As soon as he told Symonds, the coach put him right back out there. And that was where he stayed.

At Triton, Puckett started to loosen up a bit and joke around with the guys. One afternoon, he had them rolling after he showed them a new bunting style he had invented. He held the bat right in front of his face. At the last moment, he dropped it out of the way, pretending to let the ball hit him in the face and bounce out in front of the plate for a perfect bunt. The whole team was laughing so hard the players had tears running down their cheeks.

Other than being a jokester, Puckett also had a reputation for shining his shoes. He wanted to look professional at all times, mostly for the scouts. Also, his mother always told him to take care of his shoes. His family had not had the money to buy new shoes all the time. Puckett would take his spikes home after the game, wipe the dirt off, and polish them. He took care of them as if they were his finest dress shoes. At first, the guys looked at Puckett as if he were nuts. Before long, however, they too were shining their shoes. It built up their pride as a team. Years later, Puckett still took extra care of his shoes and uniform. While he was on the road, he always carried an iron for his clothes. People teased him, "You make plenty of money, Puck. Send 'em out!" Puckett explained in his autobiography, "Sure, I could afford it, but I like to iron."

Puckett had plenty of baseball highlights during that year at Triton. After the regular season, the team went to the Junior College World Series in Grand Junction, Colorado. The first game was against Seminole, Oklahoma—another great team.

Puckett led off with a line drive to right center, and he was standing on third base with his arms folded before the throw got back to the infield. The 5,500 fans in attendance went wild. Triton's outfielders caught any ball that flew their way.

Triton finished the tournament in fifth place. Puckett was on fire for the whole championship. He hit 11-for-16, with four triples and four doubles. To this day, Puckett still holds the record for hitting in that tournament. That season, he hit .472 batting leadoff, with 120 hits in 69 games, including 16 home runs (four in one game). He also had 81 RBIs and 48 stolen bases, and he threw out 20 or more runners from the outfield. At the top of his game, Puckett was voted Junior College Player of the Year for his region. In 18 months, he had gone from being a regular prospect to a hot pick. He had also gained a lot of strength since high school. He was not any taller, but he had put on 15 more pounds (7 kilograms). He was definitely ready for the Twins to come knocking at his door, again.

SIGNED TO A CONTRACT

In the spring of 1982, after the Triton season, the Minnesota Twins still had signing rights to Puckett for a few weeks. Other scouts were telling Catherine that Puckett could sign for as much as $100,000 in the June draft, so if he did not sign with the Twins, he could be assured of being drafted again. At the time, however, Puckett was not thinking much about money. He had been reading about the Twins in the newspapers. Twins owner Calvin Griffith had dumped almost all of his high-priced players after the 1981 strike. Now, he was putting together a team of young, inexpensive players. Puckett read that Griffith planned to bring these boys up and let them play for a couple of years before they became eligible for arbitration. Then, if it looked as if they would bring a high salary in arbitration, he would trade them. (Under arbitration, the player and the club submit salary figures to an arbitrator, who picks one or the other.) Puckett was not even sure if the story was true. All he wanted was to move up. If the story was true, he would have a chance to move up quickly with the Minnesota Twins.

In June, the Twins' new representative, Ellsworth Brown, showed up at Puckett's door, just as he had expected. During their first meeting, he tossed out a signing-bonus offer of $20,000. By holding out six months, Puckett's offer had shot up $14,000. He signed on the spot. Naively, Puckett thought that he would receive all the money right away. In reality, he got half at signing and half a year later. The first $10,000 (minus taxes), he gave to his mother. The next year, when he received the rest, he bought a Buick—a 1980 Skylark Limited. It was the first valuable possession Puckett ever owned.

Scorching the Minors

Shortly after signing his contract, Kirby Puckett was assigned to the Twins' Appalachian League team in Elizabethton, a small town tucked into the hills of eastern Tennessee. New players often start out on a Rookie-level or Class-A minor-league team, and then, if they are good, move their way up to Double A, Triple A, and finally the big leagues. Playing Rookie ball was just fine with Puckett. He was on his way. Part of the experience, though, was a little rough—he had to share a roach-infested apartment with two other players.

Immediately, Puckett became the leader of the team. At 22, Puckett was older than the other rookies, who were 18- and 19-year-olds just out of high school. Puckett's signing bonus of $20,000 was also much higher than what any of the other players received. These things aside, Puckett was a natural-born

Charlie Manuel, manager of the Philadelphia Phillies, tossed a ball to Kenny Lofton, who was hitting into a net during spring training in 2005. Back in 1982, Manuel was the roving minor-league hitting coach for the Minnesota Twins. Manuel knew Puckett could hit. He told him: "I don't want to work with you. I'll just mess you up."

leader, and the guys always seemed to gravitate to him. "Puck always had a gang," said Charlie Manuel, the Twins' roving minor-league hitting coach in the early 1980s, in *Kirby Puckett: Baseball's Last Warrior*. "He was electrifying."

Manuel met Puckett for the first time when the team was passing out uniforms. Puckett got his uniform and jogged onto the field for practice. Puckett was grinning while he ran and threw the ball. Manuel could tell he was having fun. Obviously, Puckett was comfortable with the game. "He stood out like a sore thumb," Manuel said, "the way he hustled, the way he played, the way he smiled. And the biggest thing was the way he could hit the ball."

Whenever Manuel was in Elizabethton, Puckett would seek him out and grill him on ways to make it to the big leagues. Manuel simply told him to get hits. Puckett knew he could do that, but he wanted to make sure. One day, Puckett asked Manuel a serious question, according to *Kirby Puckett: Baseball's Last Warrior.* "Charlie, don't you like black players?" he asked. "You never work with me on my hitting."

"You can hit," Manuel told him. "I don't want to work with you. I'll just mess you up."

As it turned out, Manuel was right. In 65 games at Elizabethton, Puckett scorched the league, batting .382, with 105 hits, 135 total bases, and 43 stolen bases. All of these statistics topped the league. He also led the league's outfielders in assists, putouts, and total chances.

Still, in the beginning of the year, the Twins were not convinced that Puckett had a strong enough arm to play center field. So they moved him to left field. Puckett did not let the switch faze him. He knew that eventually they would move him back where he belonged. And he was right.

The following fall, Puckett went to Florida to play in his first Instructional League, a camp for minor leaguers. Here, he met several coaches who would become key figures in his life. They were Tom Kelly, Cal Ermer, and Rick Stelmaszek. In the beginning, Puckett struggled. When Kelly, who was coaching Puckett's team, asked Stelmaszek which players he was most interested in checking out, Stelmaszek mentioned Puckett. "OK," Kelly agreed. "But he hasn't done much so far."

That fact did not seem to worry Stelmaszek. "Well, I'd like to see him anyway," he said.

From that day on, Puckett was on fire. He played fantastically during the six-week camp. For Puckett's sake, the timing was perfect. This camp was the first time most of the key figures in the Twins organization had seen him play. If there was any time Puckett needed to play well, it was now. Maybe his hot streak was fate. Or perhaps it had something to do with the "Kirby" tattoo he had just put on his left bicep. Either way, he suddenly started hitting the ball hard.

His showmanship landed him a spot in 1983 on the "high" Class-A team in Visalia, California—instead of with the Twins' "low" Class-A team in Kenosha, Wisconsin. And Puckett did not slow down. He started the year with a 16-game hitting streak. Despite playing a good part of the season with a hamstring injury, he batted .314 and belted nine home runs. In addition, he drove in 97 runs and stole 48 bases. In the outfield, he had just three errors and threw out 24 runners. His stellar performance earned him California League player- of-the-year honors. Puckett returned to the Instructional League that fall and finished with a .350 batting average.

The numbers Puckett posted that season were the best of any prospect in the Twins organization. Not surprisingly, Puckett thought he would be invited to the spring-training camp for major leaguers in Orlando, Florida, when camp opened in 1984. Much to his disappointment, he was not. Instead, he went to the minor-league camp in Melbourne, Florida. "I didn't figure that I'd be going to the big club in 1984," Puckett later admitted. "I just wanted to go to the big-league spring-training camp to meet all those guys. I was in awe of them, and I wanted to be one of them, if only for six weeks."

At the time, Twins minor-league director George Brophy was bound by the complicated roster rules. He had several other players to protect by placing them on the team's 40-man major-league roster. Because Puckett had less than three years of pro experience, Brophy knew he was not in danger of being stolen by another team. Therefore, he could stay in the minor-league camp. Although Puckett understood the process, he did not like it. "In any other organization, I would've been invited to the big-league camp," he said. "I understand the Twins' thinking now, but at the time I was really upset."

That year's camp was a learning experience for Puckett. He discovered that no matter how well he played, his future was still in someone else's hands—at least until he made the major leagues. As he later found out, even there, it still was most of the time.

Puckett did not let the snub scar him, though. In fact that spring, a kind of tug-of-war was going on in the Twins organization over Puckett. Charlie Manuel, now the manager at Double-A Orlando, tried to hide Puckett from Cal Ermer, who coached the higher Triple-A club in Toledo, Ohio. During split-squad spring games, Manuel sent Puckett to games he thought no one would be watching. He even jokingly offered Puckett the keys to his '65 Ford Mustang to take it for a spin during games. His plan, though, did not work. By the end of spring training, Puckett was on his way to becoming a Toledo Mud Hen.

THE JUMP TO TRIPLE A

"I do know that the jump from Class A to Triple A is a big one," Puckett admitted. Even though he hit about 15 line drives in his first 15 at-bats, he was introduced to something he had never seen before—killer sliders. A slider, sometimes called a nickel curve, is a pitch halfway between a curveball and a fastball, with more speed than a curveball. Also, the ball drops less and moves toward or away from the batter more than a curve. The extra speed can fool the hitter into thinking it is a fastball until it is too late.

Until this point, Puckett had been a free swinger. He even had a habit of helping out the pitcher by going after some bad pitches. In Triple A, it was a different game. "Man, it's going to be tough from now on," Puckett thought. It took a few weeks, but eventually Puckett learned how to hit better pitching.

Barely a month into the Mud Hens' season, he was batting just .263. For the first time in his minor-league career, he was not hitting the ball well.

One evening, Puckett and his roommate, Tack Wilson, sat watching television in a hotel room in Old Orchard Beach, Maine, near Portland. The rooms resembled an army barracks, and nestled right next to the railroad tracks, they were not too peaceful. When the trains roared past, the whole building shook. It had rained for three straight days. After hours of

THE MINOR LEAGUES

Major-league ball clubs usually send their drafted players to a minor-league team, also known as a farm team. Minor League Baseball is an umbrella organization for leagues that operate as affiliates of Major League Baseball. In these leagues, teams are generally independently owned but directly affiliated with a major-league team. Sometimes, these affiliations remain constant for many years; others may change from year to year. In some instances, a major-league club directly owns a minor-league team.

The major-league clubs use the minors to help develop a player's skills. At any time, exceptional players can be brought up from the farm team to play in the majors. Sometimes, major-league clubs use their talented farm-team players in trades with other teams in the majors.

Across the United States and Canada, 20 minor-league baseball leagues operate with 246 member clubs. The minor leagues are ranked into various classes. From lowest to highest, the levels are Rookie, Single A, Double A, and Triple A. At the Triple-A level are three leagues: the International League, the Pacific Coast League, and the Mexican League. Double A also playing cards and watching television, Puckett and Wilson were bored stiff.

In another room, Cal Ermer heard a knock at his door. It was the hotel clerk, with a message that he had a phone call from Calvin Griffith, the owner of the Minnesota Twins. Because the rooms did not have telephones, Ermer had to take the call at the front desk.

A few weeks earlier, there had been some talk between the owner and the coaches about bringing Puckett up to the

has three leagues: the Eastern League, the Southern League, and the Texas League.

Each major-league team has one Triple-A farm team, one Double-A team, at least two Single-A-level teams, and at least one Rookie team. For example, in the 2007 season, the Minnesota Twins have affiliations with the following minor-league teams:

- **Triple A: the Rochester Red Wings (Rochester, New York), International League.**
- **Double A: the New Britain Rock Cats (New Britain, Connecticut), Eastern League.**
- **Single A: the Fort Myers Miracle of the Florida State League.**
- **Single A: the Beloit Snappers (Beloit, Wisconsin), Midwest League.**
- **Rookie, Gulf Coast League Twins (Fort Myers, Florida) of the Gulf Coast League.**
- **Rookie, Elizabethton Twins (Elizabethton, Tennessee), Appalachian League (Kirby Puckett began his minor-league career on this team).**

Kirby Puckett met several coaches during his minor-league days who would play important roles in his career. One was Tom Kelly *(above)*, who was the manager of the Twins from 1986 to 2001. When the Twins were contemplating whether to promote Puckett to the majors, Kelly was one of the coaches who pushed the idea.

majors. At the time, Ermer said Puckett might not be ready for that step. Puckett had only played in the minors for two years, and had skipped Double-A ball entirely. With Puckett's rough start in Triple A, it seemed as if Ermer might have been right. Besides, if Puckett had a bad start in the majors, his confidence might be shaken, and that could ruin his ballplaying forever.

The final decision was made in a hotel in Seattle, Washington. The Twins were playing a series in Seattle before traveling down the coast to Anaheim, California. Regular center fielder Jim Eisenreich was sidelined with an illness that later was diagnosed as Tourette's syndrome. Calvin Griffith, coaches Kelly and Stelmaszek, and Billy Gardner, the Twins' manager at the time, were trying to figure out what to do. No one was happy with the performance of Darrell Brown, the team's backup center fielder. They wondered if they should take a chance on Puckett.

His statistics were unimpressive, but Kelly and Stelmaszek went out on a limb for him. "Forget those stats," they argued. "We know Puckett can go get the ball in the field. Can he hit major-league pitching? We're not sure, but he can field." So Griffith made the call to Ermer in Old Orchard Beach.

On May 6, 1984, Puckett was still sitting in his dingy room, flipping channels on the television. Then there was a knock on the door. A second later, Ermer stepped inside. He looked right at Puckett and said, "Congratulations, kid. You're going to the big show."

Puckett jumped up. "Who me?!"

"No, me," Ermer joked. "Yeah, you. Congratulations. They want you in Anaheim tomorrow afternoon. Got a flight for you in the morning already." Then, Ermer gave Puckett a little pep talk. He told Puckett that he would find it *easier* playing in the big leagues. The lights make it easier to hit, and the pitchers have more control. The fields are nicer, and the money is certainly better. In fact, Puckett's salary jumped from $900 a month to $40,000 a year. As sort of a side bet,

Ermer predicted that Puckett would get four hits in his first major-league game.

Ecstatic, Puckett first called his mother. Even though she knew he had it in him all along, she was thrilled. After they got off the phone, Catherine Puckett phoned all of Kirby's brothers and sisters. That rainy night in Maine, Puckett tried hard to sleep. All he could think about, though, was the great Twins players he was about to meet—Kent Hrbek, Gary Gaetti, and Frank Viola. Not to mention, he would be playing against the Angels—Reggie Jackson, Bobby Grich, Dick Schofield, and Doug DeCinces. Although he was scared to death, he was confident he could do the job.

As Puckett tossed and turned, he tried to repeat what Cal Ermer had told him. All these thoughts were winding around Puckett's mind. Under the fierce pounding of his heart, he hardly even noticed the room rattling because of the passing trains.

TO ANAHEIM

At 6:00 in the morning of May 7, Puckett took a flight out of Portland. He was scheduled to arrive in Anaheim at 4:00 that afternoon, after a flight change in Atlanta. When he got to Atlanta, however, he found that his flight was delayed. Before long, Puckett started to worry. He had not planned for any delays. In fact, he had not even imagined any trouble. Instead, he sat eyeing his watch in the airport, with only $10 in his pocket and no phone number to call in case of problems. Ermer had simply told him that someone would meet him at the airport in California at 4:00.

Finally at 6:00 that evening, Puckett arrived in California. As he stepped off the plane, he panned the gate area, looking for anyone who might be waiting for him. No one was there. At once, Puckett began to panic again. He probably never imagined that his dream come true could be so stressful. He decided to ask someone at the airport for help.

"Excuse me, do you know if there's anybody here to pick up Kirby Puckett with the Minnesota Twins?" he asked one of the airport workers. He stood there clenching his bags, hoping for a shred of good news.

"Sorry, I don't know anything about it," the guy replied.

At last, Puckett decided to handle the situation like any other person would—he got a cab. The only problem was he did not have enough money to get a cab. Nevertheless, he had to try. He told the cabbie that he was a minor-league ballplayer who had just gotten called up to the major leagues. Because he only had $10 with him, the cabbie would have to wait at the stadium while he went inside to get more money. Much to Puckett's amazement, the cab driver said, "No problem."

By the time they reached the stadium, the meter read $60. Still baffled that the driver could trust him, Puckett left one bag in the car while he ran inside. He carried his other bag up to the man at the door and told him who he was. "Oh yeah, yeah. Kirby Puckett," the guy said. "Come on in."

At the visiting clubhouse, Puckett found Mike Robertson, who was the traveling secretary for the Twins. Puckett told him that he needed his meal money to pay for the cab ride. Robertson laughed and explained that the team would pay for the cab. He handed Puckett a $100 bill. Without hesitation, Puckett bolted back out to the cab and told the driver to take $85. Puckett appreciated the cab driver's trust and patience. Years later, Puckett wished he had asked the cabbie for his name. "Free tickets anytime for that cab driver," he said.

When Puckett got back to the clubhouse with all of his bags, one of the coaches told him to hurry up and get dressed. Manager Billy Gardner wanted Puckett to have some batting practice. So Puckett threw on the uniform they gave him—No. 34—and walked up the ramp to the field. Puckett was surprised to see so many people in the stands. More people were in the stands for batting practice than were at most Mud Hens games. He had gone from playing in stadiums with 9,000 seats to playing in one with as many as 70,000. From down on the field, the sight of the massive ballpark was thrilling yet intimidating at the same time. Puckett began to get nervous.

During batting practice, Puckett hit the ball hard and solid—nothing spectacular, however. Then, he took a run around the bases. Gardner came over and introduced himself as the manager and commented that Puckett looked tired, a little jet-lagged.

"Not really, coach, I'm ready to go," Puckett insisted. "I'm a little tired, but I'm ready."

"No. I'll tell you what," Gardner said. "I want you to sit on the bench tonight, eat some sunflower seeds, chew some gum, relax, and watch the guys play. But tomorrow night, you'll be my starting center fielder." At first, the coaches had put Puckett in the lineup. When he showed up so late, they decided to replace him.

Puckett must have wondered what the other players were thinking as they looked him over that first night. At five-foot-eight and 175 pounds, he did not exactly have a major-league build. Some of them probably thought the organization was making a big mistake in believing this Puckett guy could be the Twins' future center fielder.

Rookie Impact

On May 8, 1984, Kirby Puckett played in his first major-league game against the California Angels. Earlier that day, Puckett called his mother to tell her he would be starting that night. "I told you so," Catherine said. "I'm proud of you. I said you were going to be a major leaguer." Before batting practice, Puckett just sat on the dugout bench, looking nervous. Then, one of baseball's legends—Reggie Jackson—walked up to Puckett and held out his hand.

"Your name's Puckett, right?" Jackson said, as detailed in *I Love This Game!*

"Yes, Mr. Jackson," Puckett answered and shook Jackson's hand. "Nice to meet you, Mr. Jackson."

"It looks like you hit them a long way," Jackson commented.

"No, just a few singles," Puckett humbly replied.

Jokingly, Jackson said, "Another singles hitter! What am I doing shaking your hand, then." Everyone close by burst out laughing.

Soon after, Puckett wasn't laughing as he stepped into the box for his first at-bat in the major leagues. He glanced up in the stands, where more than 23,000 people filled the seats. Jim Slaton stood on the pitcher's mound as Puckett pulled his bat up and nervously waited for the first pitch. With a strong swing, Puckett grounded the ball between shortstop and third base. Later, he could not remember the count. Chances are, though, it was the first pitch, because he would swing at so many of them. Shortstop Dick Schofield backhanded the ball to first base, and the throw barely beat Puckett to the bag. A bang of a hit, but he was out. As Puckett trotted back to the dugout, he thought, "Man, in Triple A, that's a hit. If this is how it's going to be in the big leagues, I'm in trouble. I'm in big trouble. I need those infield hits."

The second time he was up, Puckett was still nervous but a little more confident. He hit a single up the middle. Barely on the base, he saw the third-base coach, Tom Kelly, flash the steal sign. They had gone over the signs that afternoon. So Puckett took off and easily stole second. The next player up got a base hit behind second base. Off again, Puckett bolted past third and scored his first major-league run. Back in the dugout, the guys all patted Puckett on the back.

Next time at bat, Puckett got a single to right. He was two-for-three. The time after that, he got another base hit—three-for-four. His final time up, Puckett drove another one up the middle. That hit made him four-for-five in his first major-league game. Somebody later told Puckett that he was just the ninth player in major-league history to get four hits in his debut. At center field, Puckett caught whatever came his way, just as Kelly and Stelmaszek had promised Griffith.

In the hotel room in Old Orchard Beach, Cal Ermer had predicted Puckett's four-hit game. Watching the game that

Kirby Puckett watched the flight of the ball after getting a hit in a game against the California Angels at Anaheim Stadium. Puckett made his major-league debut on May 8, 1984, at Anaheim. He got four hits in five at-bats, the ninth player in baseball history to do so in his first game.

night, Ermer must have smiled to himself. In Anaheim, however, Puckett was so wrapped up in the excitement, he forgot about the bet. The following spring, Puckett ran into Ermer at training camp in Orlando, Florida. The two men hugged and slapped each other on the back. Then, Ermer leaned in close and whispered, "I told you right, didn't I?" It took a minute for Puckett to realize what Ermer was talking about, but finally he remembered Ermer's unbelievable prediction. Puckett laughed and yelled, "Yeah! Yeah!"

After the West Coast trip, the Twins headed back to Minnesota. The first game at the Metrodome in Minneapolis was the first time Puckett had ever seen the place, or any domed stadium, or ever even played on artificial turf. Although many players dislike artificial turf, Puckett never had a problem with it. He did take some time, however, getting used to something called "Humpball," the weird bounces and super-high hops the ball takes when it hits artificial turf.

In fact, Puckett quickly figured out how to turn the Metrodome into a home-field advantage. Most guys on the other teams wore regular steel spikes at the plate and rubber spikes in the field. The Metrodome's artificial turf is extra slick, probably from all the Vikings football games played there. The players with the steel spikes would come barreling around second base. Then, when they took their first step off the dirt area around the bag onto the turf, their feet flew out from under them—every time. That's how Puckett got a league-leading 16 assists that first year—by throwing behind the guys who fell down on a big turn at second base. Puckett, on the other hand, never had trouble because he batted in rubber cleats. In truth, he never needed steel cleats anyway, because he didn't "dig in" at the plate. The big, strong guys who hit home runs wear steel cleats for this purpose. Puckett, though, liked to stay on top of the dirt, hit the ball, and bolt out of there as soon as possible. He did not want his cleats holding him back.

At the end of his first year, Puckett had a .296 batting average, with plenty of bunts. His lead in assists helped earn him spots on most of the All-Rookie teams, and he finished third in the voting for Rookie of the Year. That year, Alvin Davis, a first baseman for Seattle, won the award, with his 27 homers. Puckett's rookie year pleased the Twins. As Rick Stelmaszek said in *Kirby Puckett: Baseball's Last Warrior*, "We weren't looking for a star when Puckett came up from the

TOO MANY STRIKEOUTS

One of the standard jokes on the Twins was the white mask, or hood, that was awarded to anyone who struck out three times in one game. In baseball terminology, a "K" is a strikeout, so three strikeouts is three Ks—"KKK." (Members of the Ku Klux Klan racial hate group wear white hooded masks when they appear in public.) Although Kirby Puckett could see how an outsider might think that the mask was in bad taste, that was what the mask was called. In his first year with the Twins, Puckett got the hood against the Texas Rangers. Ten years later, Puckett vowed to trash the hood, mainly because he thought it was too negative. "You get two strikeouts in the game, and the next thing you know, you're worrying about getting that mask," he said in his autobiography. Once a person had the hood, he wanted to get rid of it. Of course, though, he would not want someone else to have it, either.

The Twins pitchers used to have a sombrero they awarded to any pitcher who gave up four homers in a game or any hitter who struck out four times. Bert Blyleven—"Gopher Bert" because he gave up so many homers (a gopher pitch is a pitch that leads to a home run)—finally threw the hat away. Puckett thought that was a good idea.

minors. We were just looking for a warm body to replace Darrell Brown," the former center fielder. With a solid rookie year, Puckett was on his way to becoming a whole lot more than just a "warm body." If his ballplaying did not prove it, his salary increase did. For his rookie year, the Twins gave Puckett the standard one-year deal of $40,000, plus a $10,000 bonus to stay out of winter ball. (They were afraid he might get hurt during the off-season.) After having a pretty good year, Puckett expected some sort of a raise, but he really had no leverage. He could not participate in arbitration for another two years. Nevertheless, the Twins boosted his pay to $120,000, plus $10,000 in incentives. This amount was more than the team had ever paid a second-year player.

HOME RUN SILENCE

On April 22, 1985, Puckett hit his first home run in the major leagues, off Matt Young of the Mariners. The 340-foot (104-meter) hit sailed all the way to the second row of the left-field seats in the Metrodome, just beyond the stadium's plexiglass wall. Oddly, his teammates greeted his accomplishment with complete silence and straight faces. Puckett had heard about the "silent treatment" when a player smacks his first home run. A couple of minutes went by, and still nobody talked.

"Geez, guys, weren't you watching?" Puckett asked, breaking what seemed like an unbearably long silence. "Don't you know the Puck finally hit a homer?" Finally, his teammates gave in and congratulated him with slaps on the back.

The season started out slowly for the Twins, but they had high hopes. Many sports writers had picked Minnesota to win the American League West handily that year. The team was young, energetic, and skilled, and the division did not have a powerhouse team. The players, though, were not playing up to their potential. By mid-June, the Twins were still seven or eight games out of first place. As it usually goes, when the players do not perform, the manager gets blamed.

Pictured here in a photo from 1984, Kirby Puckett had plenty to smile about that rookie season. He batted .296 and came in third in voting for the American League Rookie of the Year. After the season, the Minnesota Twins raised his salary from $40,000 to $120,000 plus $10,000 in incentives—the most the team had ever paid a second-year player.

In early June, the papers reported that Carl Pohlad, the new owner of the Twins, had promised not to fire Billy Gardner, despite the sluggish start. Two weeks after those reports, though, Pohlad fired Gardner. The news came as a huge shock to Puckett.

According to the newspapers, Gardner's problem was that he waited for the team to get the big hits from Kent Hrbek or

Tom Brunansky. Also, he was not a great communicator with the players. Once, Gardner called motivation a college word he did not understand, meaning he did not believe motivation would win games. The night before he was fired, however, Gardner got himself kicked out of the game to "motivate" the players. His plan worked, and the team came from three runs behind to beat Kansas City. Unfortunately, the move did not do him any good.

Naturally, Puckett liked Gardner, because he was one of the few people in the Twins organization who had been willing to take a chance on him. On the afternoon he was fired, Gardner walked into the clubhouse to clean out his locker and say goodbye to everyone. When he got to Puckett, he wished him good luck and said he would be following Puckett's career.

During the 1985 season, Puckett hit three more home runs, 29 doubles, and 13 triples. He drove in 74 runs, and had a .288 batting average. One disappointment Puckett faced was coming up one hit short of 200 that year. The other letdown was that the Twins never climbed back into the pennant race, even after hiring a new manager, Ray Miller. They finished 77–85, a long way behind the Kansas City Royals.

Toward the end of the season, a little bright spot occurred in Puckett's career. Many of his 199 hits had been to right field. He had always had an inside-out stroke, sending the ball to right field. As he told Reggie Jackson, he was a singles hitter. During batting practice, late in the season, some of the guys teased Puckett about being just a right-field hitter—not being able to hit home runs. In truth, for the most part, Puckett agreed with them. Still, he decided to prove his teammates wrong and proceeded to hit 10 home runs in a row, right then and there. They were not just fly balls either, just beyond the outfield wall. They were bombs. This output during batting practice gave Puckett a lot to think about during the off-season and sparked a dramatic change in his hitting stats the following spring.

FINDING TONYA

One night in 1985, Puckett and some friends from the Twins went to a nightclub. The restaurant was upstairs, with a dance floor downstairs. The guys were downstairs joking around, when a group of women walked through the front door. One woman caught Puckett's eye, so he waved to her. Embarrassed, she responded with a half-wave. A while later, Puckett got her attention and motioned to her to come over by him. That move surprised her, and she shot him an obvious "Give me a break!" look. Puckett was persistent and eventually managed to coax her over to his table. Then, without saying a word, she flashed him a captivating smile.

She introduced herself as Tonya Hudson. Then, Puckett introduced himself. As their conversation continued, it was clear she did not know who Kirby Puckett was. Puckett was almost dumbfounded. He was having a good year. So he added that he was "Kirby Puckett—of the Minnesota Twins." At least Hudson knew who the Twins were, but she still did not recognize his name. She admitted that she was not really a baseball fan. However, she found it funny that he made a point to let her know exactly who he was. Years later, she still teased him about it.

As they talked, Puckett learned that Hudson worked at a jewelry store and as a supervisor at a clothing store and that she had quit a third job because it was too much for her to handle. Most nights, she stayed at home with her parents, with whom she lived. Finally, Puckett introduced her to his friends as "his girlfriend." Hudson threw him a glare that said, "Who are you kidding?"

After a while, Hudson took Puckett over to her table to meet her group—her sister Nicko, her Aunt Leslie, and a few friends. Puckett offered to buy Nicko a drink, and she replied, "No, you don't have to buy me a drink. I have my own money." After fishing around in her purse for a couple of minutes, she realized that she did not have her wallet. Finally, a little embarrassed, she said, "Well, I guess you can buy me that drink after all." They all had a good laugh.

As the night went on, Puckett became bolder. Eventually, he told Hudson that she was going to be his wife. He could not even believe his own words, and it was obvious that Hudson did not believe him either. She thought he was just feeding her a line. When the club was closing, Puckett offered to give Hudson a ride back to her Aunt Leslie's house, where she had left her car. The suggestion led to some serious conversation among the women. They were not sure they wanted Hudson getting into a car with a stranger, even if it was Kirby Puckett of the Minnesota Twins. Finally, Leslie wrote down Puckett's license plate number and told him that he had exactly *10 minutes* to get her niece to her house. If he was not there by that time, she would call the police.

Puckett drove pretty quickly to Aunt Leslie's house. On the way, he once again told Hudson that she would end up being his wife. When they got to the house, Puckett took down her phone number and asked her out to lunch the next day. (He had a night game, so he couldn't ask her out to dinner.) He told her one more time that she was his future wife.

By this point, Hudson had listened to enough of this talk. "You know," she said, "if you marry someone you should be in love with that person. I don't know you. You don't know me. You don't know what I'm like. I could be crazy. So you shouldn't keep on saying that right now." Again, Puckett assured her that he had never done anything like this before. Of course, he had been on dates, but he had never had a steady girlfriend. She agreed to go out with him the next day.

After a few dates, Hudson decided that Puckett should meet her mother. The three of them met downtown at an Arby's. Although Puckett just had a Coke, he wanted to pay for everyone. Mrs. Hudson refused, saying that a mother does not let the kids pay. Immediately, Puckett thought of his own

Kirby and Tonya Puckett and their children, Catherine and Kirby, Jr., joked around in 1997 in their home in Minnesota. Kirby Puckett met Tonya Hudson in 1985, and they married a year later.

mother. The only way he could get her to take money from him was if he left it on the kitchen table and ran out of her apartment. Sometimes, Puckett sent her money by Federal Express, so she would have to accept it. Puckett always wanted to buy Catherine a house, but when he could finally afford it, she would not even accept a condo. So Puckett knew it was best not to argue with Tonya's mother. Almost instantly, Puckett and Mrs. Hudson hit it off. Years later, she sometimes joined Puckett and the guys for card games. Because the Hudsons have four daughters and no sons, they later considered Puckett the son they never had.

Then, the time came for Puckett to meet Tonya's father and the rest of the family. They planned the get-together for 1:00 on a Sunday afternoon, when Tonya would be at work. She would show up later. Puckett made sure he was there on time. When Puckett strolled around the corner, he found Mr. Hudson working in the yard. They had barely introduced themselves when the rest of the family filed out the front door. Puckett never had any trouble getting along with people, so he was not too nervous.

On September 26, 1985, Puckett proposed to Tonya and slipped an impressive diamond ring on her finger. That night, he blasted a long hit. To top it all off, the Twins won the game.

The wedding took place on November 1, 1986. They tried to plan an average-size wedding, but by the time it was over, they both wished they had had a much smaller affair. Better yet, they wished they had just gone to Las Vegas. They had no honeymoon after the wedding because they were busy getting ready to move into their new home in Brooklyn Park, Minnesota. Before the wedding, they had lived in the Hudsons' house for almost the whole 1986 season. After they got engaged, Mr. Hudson thought it was the best arrangement while the couple waited for their house to be built. When Puckett showed up with all of his belongings, Mrs. Hudson made a big deal about all the "junk" he owned. Making Minnesota his full-time home was a big decision for Puckett. To Tonya, it just made sense. She lived in Minnesota, and he played there. After some thought, Puckett decided that she was right—Minnesota was home.

From Singles to Homers

After the 1985 season, Kirby Puckett hired Ron Shapiro, an attorney and agent who lives in Baltimore, Maryland. He represented ballplayers like Cal Ripken, Jr., Eddie Murray, and other big names. Puckett met Shapiro in a hotel lobby in Cleveland, and they clicked at once. Shortly after, Puckett asked Shapiro to represent him. Puckett knew who the strongest agents in the business were, and Shapiro was one of them. More important, Shapiro had a more quiet style, and Puckett did not want his contract negotiations to be on the front page of the newspaper.

Immediately, Puckett appreciated Shapiro's work. For the 1986 season, still without arbitration, Puckett received $230,000 plus incentives. In two years, he had gone from a salary of $40,000 a year to almost $200,000 more per year. He had reached the big money and was ready for a big year.

For the Twins, the 1986 season was even worse than 1985 had been. They finished 20 games under .500, 21 games behind the California Angels, and barely ahead of Seattle in the cellar (last place) of the American League West. For Puckett, however, it was a huge year and a whole new experience, because he started to hit home runs on a regular basis. He hit 31 home runs in 1986. Interestingly, Puckett was the only player in major-league history to have a season with no home runs in at least 500 at-bats—his rookie year, 1984—and then come back in a later season to hit more than 30. The season transformed Puckett from a singles hitter to a guy with a powerful bat.

When Puckett was in the minors, he met Tony Oliva, another roving hitting instructor for the Twins. Oliva would travel to each minor-league town for a week or so to work with the hitters. Back then, Puckett and Oliva hit the ball pretty much the same—inside-out swing, no great power. Puckett always hit to score runs, while working on a high average. Oliva had told Puckett that he had the body and the power to hit 20 home runs a year. At that time, Puckett just laughed at Oliva and thought, "Yeah, sure, Tony." After Puckett hit those 10 homers during batting practice in 1985, he began to change his mind.

Until this point, Puckett was comfortable just putting the ball in play and using his speed to get on base. At the same time, he knew deep down that he had more power. He just did not want to mess up his basic stroke trying to hit home runs. Oliva explained that hitting for more power could actually help his average. Outfielders would have to play deeper when Puckett was up to bat. They would not be counting on him to hit the ball to right field. In turn, they would have to spread out, leaving more holes in the outfield.

So in the spring of 1986, Puckett decided to kick his batting up a notch and add some power. In the off-season, he had lifted weights. He was ready to experiment in training. Puckett felt he was open to advice and change, but he did not want to do anything that would shatter his confidence. Both Oliva and Puckett knew that changing the style and thinking of a successful ballplayer is tough to do. If Puckett were to go three or four games without a hit while trying something new, the experiment would probably be over.

Within a couple of weeks, Oliva and Puckett had developed his high leg kick. They worked early and late every day. To have a good high kick when batting, the player must first shift his weight to his back leg, then push the weight forward. When a player hits the ball, and even if he does not, everything goes *into* the pitch. With that kick, timing is key. If a player kicks too early, he will have to hesitate, which will not help. He still *might* be able to do something with the pitch. Too late, however, and it is strike three. The timing has to be perfect, but the player cannot think about it at the plate. It has to be automatic. All that the player can focus on is hitting the ball, and hard.

At first, the transition was not easy, but day after day, Puckett could feel his technique getting better. He started to hit the ball hard to left field as well as to right, depending on where the ball was thrown. Puckett left spring-training camp charged up and full of confidence. His confidence got a boost in an early game when his home-run ball hit a police cruiser way out in the parking lot. In April, he was the American League Player of the Month, leading the majors in homers with nine and batting .389.

One home run was particularly special. He was playing at Yankee Stadium. The first time he ever walked out of the visitors' dugout there he got chills. Two years later, he was still in awe. The stadium is one of the most famous sports venues in the world. On this day in 1986, he had hit the ball solidly in his first at-bats. Two of his long fly balls, though, were caught on the warning track in left center, which, at the time, was 411 feet from home plate. After the second long out, Ray Miller came up to Puckett and said, "This park's too big for you."

Kirby Puckett used a high leg kick to get more power at the plate. He worked with hitting coach Tony Oliva during spring training in 1986 to develop the kick. It must have worked. That year, Puckett hit 31 home runs, becoming the first player to hit more than 30 home runs in a year after hitting none in an earlier season.

Puckett did not say a word. Although the Twins joked around a lot, he was not sure that Miller's comment was a joke. In the seventh inning, with a 3-2 count, Puckett swung at a knee-high fastball. "You could have heard that *Crack!* a mile away," Puckett recalled in his autobiography. Some people say the ball flew 500 feet (152 meters). Puckett rounded the bases. When he got back to the dugout, all of his teammates were jumping up and down. When Miller stuck out his hand to congratulate him, Puckett said, "I'm not shaking your hand. Too big for me, huh? There's your 'too big.'"

NUMBER THREE

As the All-Star Game got closer that summer, Puckett was in the running to make the team for the first time. He really wanted to nab the honor. The year before, he watched Tom Brunansky play in the All-Star Game at the Metrodome. In 1986, Puckett wanted to be the one going to the game at the Astrodome in Houston. Late in June, he was still fourth in the voting for outfielders, behind Rickey Henderson, Dave Winfield, and Reggie Jackson, and only the top three are guaranteed to make the team as starters. By early July, however, he was only about 700 votes behind Jackson for the third slot. The newspapers boasted that Puckett could be the first Twin to start on the team since Roy Smalley started at shortstop in 1979. Much to Puckett's delight, he would also earn a $10,000 bonus. With a .340 batting average, 16 homers, and almost 50 RBIs, he thought he deserved it.

Suddenly, he fell behind by 7,000 votes and figured he was out of the running. So when Ray Miller gave him the news that he had made the team, Puckett was overwhelmed.

In Houston, Puckett was the leadoff hitter in the game, meaning he would be the first player to face Dwight Gooden—the opposing pitcher. To reporters, Puckett joked that, if Gooden punched him out on strikes, he hoped the fans were out getting their food at the concession stands. If he managed a hit, however, he hoped they were in their seats to see it. When the time came, Puckett cracked a ground ball up the middle on the first pitch for a single. He was the only

☆☆☆☆☆☆

KIRBY PUCKETT'S CHARITY WORK

Many baseball stars use some of their wealth and prestige to help the community. Kirby Puckett gave back to his fans in several ways. In 1985, drug indictments came down in baseball. That summer, the Twins had signed Steve Howe, who had battled a well-publicized problem with cocaine. In September, Howe disappeared one weekend while the Twins were in Cleveland. Right after, he appeared on the news program *Nightline* to discuss drugs and baseball, and two days later, he admitted he had slipped back into taking drugs and asked to be released from the team. At the request of management, the Twins' players agreed to be tested for drugs the next spring.

The incident got Puckett thinking. He hated to see guys ruin their careers and their lives over drugs. The problem in baseball, however, paled in comparison to the drug problems at the Robert Taylor Homes in Chicago, where Puckett grew up. So Puckett and his wife, Tonya, decided to take action in Minnesota to help youngsters stay away from drugs. They became involved with the Partnership for a Drug Free Minnesota, a program founded by Skip Humphrey, then the state's attorney general. The idea of the program was to give kids other activities to do, rather than just preach to them to keep away from drugs. The partnership created various projects, such as having the youths put together public service announcements for their schools. Each project earned points for the

American League team member to play the whole game. The coach later admitted that, if he kept Puckett in the whole time, the team would win the game, and it wanted to win. The American League had not won the All-Star Game in three

school. The school that earned the most points won tickets to a Twins game and a big picnic outside.

The Pucketts traveled to different schools during the off-season. They encouraged the kids to get involved with the program. Kirby would tell the students about the place where he grew up. He explained that his life was proof that a person can stay away from drugs and really go places.

Later in his career, Puckett held the Annual Kirby Puckett Eight-Ball Invitational Pool Tournament, which benefited the Children's Heart Fund, based in Minnesota. This organization has brought hundreds of children to the United States for heart surgery. It also works to improve cardiac-care programs in hospitals overseas. For years, Puckett was also involved with the Make-A-Wish Foundation, like many other ballplayers, athletes, and celebrities. Through the program, a child with a life-threatening illness makes a wish, and the foundation works to make it happen.

In addition, Puckett sometimes bought a block of 500 tickets for youngsters from community centers. Normally, these children would not have been able to afford to go to a ball game. He also provided hot dogs and Cokes for them at the game. Puckett enjoyed giving out tickets to these groups, which often served minority children. He wanted to see more minorities in the seats at the Metrodome.

Kirby Puckett had some prowess in hitting another kind of ball with another kind of stick—a pool cue. Here, he played billiards in November 1996 during his charity tournament to benefit the Children's Heart Fund. Puckett and his wife, Tonya, reached out in many ways to help in the community.

years and had not won many in the years before that. Thanks to Puckett's help, the American League did win, 3-2.

Shortly after the All-Star Game, Puckett got one of the biggest shocks of his career. As recounted in *I Love This Game!*, Ray Miller called Puckett into his office and said, "You know, Puck, sometimes it's good to hear this directly: Maybe you don't realize how talented you are, how much the other club respects and fears your ability. I'm coming from the other side. I know. I'm telling you, they just don't know how to get you out." Puckett was blown away. The last thing he expected to hear from the manager was an outpouring of compliments. Then, Miller added, "Congratulations, kid."

Puckett was confused. "Congratulations on what?" he asked.

"You're my No. 3 hitter from now on," Miller said.

The third batter is supposed to be the team's best hitter. Puckett was astounded. He did not quite believe he was the best hitter, not with guys like Kent Hrbek, Gary Gaetti, and Tom Brunansky on the team. By the third time Miller repeated himself, the news finally started to sink in. At the time, Puckett was unsure of the decision. After all, he was just getting comfortable in the majors. He may have been confident as a leadoff hitter, but he was not exactly sure how he would do as the No. 3 hitter.

As a team, however, the Twins did not have much to lose. At the All-Star break, their record was 37–51. With such a strong team, this baffled Puckett. Gary Gaetti was among the league leaders in home runs and RBIs, and rookie second baseman Steve Lombardozzi was in the running for a Gold Glove. Still, the wins were not coming, and that fact meant they would get a new manager. After a little more than a year as manager, Ray Miller was replaced by Tom Kelly on September 12.

Even though the Twins were out of the '86 pennant race, August 19 was a memorable night in Boston. Puckett went three-for-four, giving him the leading batting average over Wade Boggs, at .349. Also that night, Hrbek, Gaetti, and Puckett all nailed their twenty-fifth homers of the year. With this kind of hitting, it was a mystery that the team was not winning more games. Puckett could not keep up his amazing batting pace, however, and his average slipped the rest of the season. He finished with a batting average of .328, third behind Wade Boggs (.357) and Don Mattingly (.352). He did not stay at No. 3 in the batting lineup, either, switching back to leadoff most of the time.

The 1986 season was not a total loss. Puckett won a Gold Glove award for his play in center field. Each year, the award is given to a major-league player who excels in the field. An award goes to one player at each position in each league, 18 Gold Gloves in all. Teammate Gary Gaetti also earned a Gold Glove that year for his performance at third base. With the award came a $10,000 bonus, which Puckett was happy to collect.

In Puckett's mind, earning a Gold Glove was just as monumental as coming in first in batting average. "Homers are great," he said in his autobiography, "but what about robbing other guys of homers? Just as much fun, believe me."

Unfortunately, Puckett entered the 1987 season on a sore note. Because of a change in major-league rules, he still was not eligible for arbitration. Under the new rules, he needed three complete years to qualify. With arbitration, Puckett would have been able to get at least a $750,000 salary, maybe more, given his stats. The first offer came in at $265,000, a $35,000 raise over his 1986 salary. Ron Shapiro and Puckett thought that the offer was unfair, considering Gaetti and Hrbek were earning around $1 million apiece. After some debate, the Twins came up with a second offer of $365,000. One day later, Puckett signed a contract for $365,000, plus $100,000 in incentives. He was looking forward to 1988, however, when he could earn as much as the other top players.

The Road to Number One

On Opening Day at the Metrodome in 1987, two questions circled in Kirby Puckett's mind: Could he do as well as he had in 1986? And could the Twins do better? Of his 223 hits the previous season, one-third were for extra bases—37 doubles, 6 triples, and 31 homers. Before 1986, Puckett would never have imagined that kind of extra-base hitting. He wondered if he could keep the power going.

Puckett had one big advantage. He was a "bad ball hitter," meaning he could handle pitches that were not even in the strike zone. The opposite type of player is called a "mistake hitter." In almost every at-bat, a player has a chance of seeing at least one good pitch to hit. That pitch is a mistake. Puckett could hammer the mistakes, but he loved to make the bad pitches hurt, too. In 1986, instead of just taking a mistake for a single, he was not afraid to try to pull it over the fence for a home run.

The Twins had the makings of a great team. Newcomer Dan Gladden would play left field and lead off. Tom Brunansky was in right field. Puckett, of course, had earned another year in center field. Playing the infield were Kent Hrbek, Steve Lombardozzi, Greg Gagne, and Gary Gaetti. Randy Bush and rookie Mark Davidson helped fill in for the outfielders, and Al Newman held up the infield. As pitchers, the Twins had Frank Viola, Bert Blyleven, Mike Smithson, Les Straker, and knuckle-balling Joe Niekro. Jeff Reardon was the team's closer. Sharing the job of catcher were Tim Laudner and Tom Nieto. The team had base hitters, power hitters, and hitters who did both, like Puckett. The Twins may not have been the most glamorous team in the league, but there was no doubt their lineup could win games.

As hoped, the season started out with a bang. In the opener against Oakland, Puckett cranked out a homer, a double, and a single. In the outfield, he took some extra bases, and maybe even a home run, away from Mickey Tettleton. With the score tied at 4-4 in the tenth inning, Tettleton hit a high-arcing ball toward the wall in center. Puckett jumped so high to catch the ball that his armpit was above the top of the seven-foot-high wall. Tettleton kicked second base in disgust. In the Metrodome stands, the fans jumped to their feet to give Puckett his first standing "O" of the season. Then, the Twins came back to win in the bottom half of the inning.

During another game in Oakland, Puckett and Randy Bush met with a near disaster. During the game, a routine fly ball headed toward right center. Puckett ran over for the catch, hollering "I got it!" all the way. Bush, who was playing right field instead of Brunansky that night, was yelling for it, too. Puckett called him off. With all the noise in Oakland's stadium, Bush did not hear him. Focused only on the ball, they both arrived under it at the same time. Being taller, Bush caught the ball over

Puckett's head, while Puckett smacked into him. At the end of the play, Bush was still standing, but Puckett fell to the ground, holding his knee.

Puckett looked up to see Bush throwing in the ball, and said, "Way to go, man. You caught it."

Noticing Puckett on the ground, Bush asked, "Puck, are you all right?"

"No. I'm hurt," Puckett said.

Realizing that the ball technically should have been Puckett's (it was in center field), Bush began to panic. "Puck, you gotta get up! My career could be over! You've *got* to get up!"

By this time, Tom Kelly and Dick Martin, the trainer, were on their way out. Knowing that Bush was a bit anxious, and being the jokester of the team, Puckett laid it on extra thick, rolling around as if he was in horrible pain. Finally, Puckett decided he was all right, Martin said so, too, and Puckett popped up and ran off the field. Bush harped on Puckett all the way back to the dugout, "Man, you can't do that to me, Puck."

In August, the Twins prepared to play the Milwaukee Brewers. The Twins were heading toward the division championship, even though Puckett had been struggling with his hitting. He even struck out three times in the All-Star Game that year, which embarrassed him. So, he was hoping to bring his game back.

Puckett's sister June lived in Milwaukee, and every time Puckett came through town, he made sure to stop over for some of her good home cooking. June picked up Puckett and teammate Al Newman at the hotel and brought them over for a feast of fried chicken and homemade fries, Puckett's favorite. After the meal, Puckett and Newman left for the stadium. On the way, Puckett joked that he wished he could hit as well as his sister could cook. When they got to the park, Tony Oliva hollered at Puckett to come over and talk about his hitting. Puckett knew he had been on again, off again over the past few months. He was not feeling confident at the plate, lunging at the ball and

Among the Kirby Puckett memorabilia at the Baseball Hall of Fame in Cooperstown, New York, is a bat he used in 1987, when he got 10 hits in two games against the Milwaukee Brewers. In one of the games, he hit two home runs, two doubles, and two singles. In the other game, Puckett went four-for-five. The other items here are his cap from the 1993 All-Star Game and a glove he used in spring training.

swinging at pitches that were not just bad—which was what he usually did—but terrible. For some reason, that day felt different, though.

"Tony, man, I feel great today," Puckett said. "Check me out today. I don't know what it is." Still, they talked for a while about staying with the ball, and other basic advice. Then, it was Puckett's turn to take batting practice. Sure enough, every ball Puckett hit during practice was a bullet. He punched them down the right-field line, to left-center, and to center field. That day, a Saturday, Puckett went four-for-five, with two home runs and two singles. That was great hitting, but nothing sensational. Even so, the game boosted Puckett's confidence.

On Sunday, Puckett had that same great feeling. He told Oliva that he felt as if he was still in the zone. "That's good! That's good!" Oliva said. Each time Puckett got up to the plate—crack! crack! crack!, one after another. By the ninth inning, he was five-for-five, including one homer. With two outs, Greg Gagne swung and missed on a third strike, but the ball rolled to the screen. He took off to first and beat the throw. Puckett had one more chance at bat. Dan Plesac was on the mound, and he threw a fastball low and away. It was a tough pitch, but Puckett kicked his leg and swung. The ball rocketed to right field for a home run. Later, Plesac said that people could have been knocked unconscious by that shot. The hit was so incredible that Brewers fans actually gave Puckett a standing ovation.

That game, Puckett went six-for-six, with two homers, two doubles, and two singles. In those two games, he was 10-for-11, with four home runs—two to left field, two to right. His 14 total bases in Sunday's game (eight bases total on the home runs, four bases for the two doubles, and two bases for the singles) set a single-game record for the Twins. The 10 hits in two consecutive nine-inning games set an American League record. As another high point, the wins in Milwaukee put the Twins back in front of the Oakland A's in the American League West.

Every ball that Puckett hit that weekend was hard, on the meat of the barrel. He had never felt so on fire before, and it never happened again. He also stole a grand slam from Robin Yount in the sixth inning of Sunday's game. At Milwaukee County Stadium, the fence has a lower cushion section, and above that, a strip of chain-link fencing. Puckett's glove reached above the chain-link to catch that home-run ball. Puckett was always careful to give his sister June credit for his incredible weekend, because it all started off with her fried chicken.

The Twins sewed up the American League West title with a win over the Texas Rangers, with a week to go in the season. By that time, everyone on the team was playing with amazing confidence. After the final game, the team had a wild celebration in the clubhouse. Then, Puckett did something sort of

KIRBY PUCKETT'S BATS

During Kirby Puckett's hot streak against the Milwaukee Brewers in 1987, he broke his bat on a swing. The bat was a C243, the same model used by Rod Carew, a former player on the Twins and the Angels. Afterward, Puckett shipped a bat he used during those two games to the Baseball Hall of Fame in Cooperstown, New York, for an exhibit. Most fans do not understand how much thought goes into what bat to use.

When Puckett made his debut in the big leagues, he used a light bat, 34 inches (86 centimeters) long and 31 ounces (879 grams), because he was just a base hitter. At that time, he did not know much about hitting home runs. Then, in 1986, the year Puckett started to rack up the homers, he switched to Carew's longer, heavier model, which was 35 inches (89 centimeters) long and 33 ounces (936 grams). To most people, two ounces may not seem like much, but it makes a tremendous difference to a hitter. With 31 homers in 1986, it made all the difference for Puckett.

Eventually, Puckett developed his own model, the P339. It had the same specifications as Carew's bat. The "339" represented Puckett's batting average when he won the batting title in 1989.

strange. Al Newman, Mark Davidson, and Puckett had formed a club called "The Dawgs." Puckett started the club by always saying, "You gotta be a 'dawg' to play this game," meaning play dirty, play hurt, play sick, play even if you don't feel like coming to the park. They each had two "Dawg" T-shirts—one red, one blue—with "YOU GOTTA BE A DAWG" on the back. While celebrating the division title in Texas, the Dawgs all got down on their hands and knees and started to bark. It was all part of the excitement. They were going to the playoffs.

Perhaps The Dawgs was a fitting name for the Twins' club. The team had been the underdogs all season and still were going into the playoffs. No one really expected the Twins to win. Their record of 85–77 was the worst of the four division champions and only the ninth-best in the major leagues. The experts pointed out all kinds of negatives about the Twins. After the division clincher in Texas, they lost five straight games to end the season on a low note. The Detroit Tigers—considered the best team in baseball and the team the Twins would face in the American League Championship Series—included several players from the 1984 World Series-winning team. On the Twins, only two players had postseason experience—pitcher Bert Blyleven and Don Baylor. Although the team had a great home record (56–25), it had a terrible record on the road (29–52).

WORLD SERIES

On October 7, the Twins faced the Detroit Tigers at the Metrodome in Game 1 of the American League Championship Series (ALCS). With the Tigers' history, most people believed the series would be no contest. The Twins would obviously lose. Of course, Minnesota fans felt differently, sitting in the stands waving their now-famous "homer hankies." That day, the Twins proved the rest of baseball wrong, winning 8-5 behind Gary Gaetti's two home runs and Tom Brunansky's three RBIs. They did, in fact, belong in the championship series, no matter what their record was. Puckett went one-for-four in the game, but his double was a big hit, bringing home Dan Gladden to tie the score in the eighth inning. Don Baylor followed with a single that scored Puckett and put Minnesota ahead for good.

Their victory was especially important to the Twins for another reason. The win was against Tiger pitching ace Doyle Alexander, who had been 9–0 since joining Detroit in an August trade. As Twins manager Tom Kelly said, "We proved he was human."

In Game 2, played at the Metrodome on October 8, the Twins beat Detroit again, this time against another superb pitcher—Jack Morris. At the end of the game, the score was 6-3. This time, Puckett was hitless in four at-bats. Gladden again delivered for the Twins with a two-run single.

After Game 2, the series shifted to Detroit. Now, Minnesota had to figure out how to turn that miserable road record upside down. Although they were down two games in the series, the Tigers probably believed their luck was about to change. Again, Puckett struggled at the plate, going zero-for-five. On October 10, Game 3 belonged to the Tigers, with a 7-6 win.

Until Game 4, Puckett had not been playing well. It was impossible, though, to keep him down for the entire series. This time, Puckett had two hits, including a home run. He scored twice to help the Twins take a 5-3 win. "My teammates know it's just a matter of time," Puckett said. "I just play hard and let the chips fall where they may." Leading the championship series, three games to one, the Twins hoped they could keep rolling with one more win on the road. On the afternoon of October 12, Minnesota brought a quick end to the series, pounding the Tigers with a 9-5 win. A four-run second inning did most of the damage, fueled by Brunansky's double that scored two runs. Puckett went two-for-six and drove in a run.

The visiting clubhouse in Detroit was too small for The Dawgs to get down on the floor and bark. They did have enough room to celebrate with champagne, though. And there was plenty to cheer about. Not only did the Twins clinch the American League Championship Series, they earned a trip to the World Series.

The championship series was an incredible victory, but the battle was far from over. In the World Series, the Twins would take on the St. Louis Cardinals. The Cardinals had just survived a grueling seven-game series against the San Francisco Giants. Once again, the Twins were the underdogs. "We were supposed to lose, of course," Puckett said, "but we didn't pay any attention to the prediction."

Back at the Metrodome for Game 1 on October 17, Gladden pounded a grand slam, sparking a seven-run fourth inning. Puckett had a quiet start to the series, going one-for-five. Still, the Twins throttled the Cardinals, 10-1. Twins pitcher Frank Viola took the victory, throwing eight solid innings. In Game 2, the Twins defeated St. Louis, 8-4, thanks to Tim Laudner's two-run single and a 420-foot (128-meter) home run. Puckett went one-for-four and scored one run.

For the next three games, the World Series moved to Busch Stadium in St. Louis, Missouri. Here, the series took a turn for the worse. St. Louis's pitchers held Minnesota's mighty bats to five runs and 18 hits in three games, giving the Cardinals a three-games-to-two lead in the World Series. On the road, Puckett really struggled, with only two hits in 11 trips to the plate. He was outraged by the way the Twins got stomped on. "We were hopping mad after the showing," Puckett said. "No way this team gets 18 hits in three games."

After Game 5, Puckett decided it was time for him to take action. He just could not understand why he was not hitting the ball. Naturally, he took some extra batting practice, but he also tried something he seldom did. He watched some videos of the previous games. Throughout baseball, Puckett had a reputation for being a free swinger. Expecting him to be eager to swing, the pitchers threw all kinds of junk way off the plate.

After the Twins won Game 1 of the 1987 World Series, Kirby Puckett congratulated pitcher Frank Viola. The Twins were underdogs in the series against St. Louis, but they easily defeated the Cardinals in the first game, 10-1. Puckett was one-for-five in the game.

Naturally, Puckett played into their trap. When he watched the videos, he realized how overeager he had been.

Fortunately, Game 6 came back to Minnesota. On his first at-bat against Cardinals pitcher John Tudor, Puckett waited, waited, and waited. Finally, he smacked a single to left field and drove in Gladden. In the fifth inning, Don Baylor nailed a two-run homer. Kent Hrbek hit a grand slam in the sixth, helping the Twins put up eight runs in those two innings alone. Puckett went four-for-four, scoring four runs. His performance on October 24 tied the World Series record for runs scored in a single series game. The Twins smoked the Cardinals, 11-5, and were ready to settle the championship with one last game.

The deciding game took place on October 25. Again, Puckett played a key role. In the fifth inning, the Twins were trailing, 2–1. Before Puckett came up to bat, the Cardinals' manager switched pitchers, from left-handed Joe Magrane to hard-throwing right-hander Danny Cox. Typically, Puckett liked to bat against left-handed pitchers, so he understood the change. Cox threw hard on his first pitch, but Puckett was ready. He hammered a double to right center, scoring Greg Gagne, to tie the game. The crowd of 55,367 in the Metrodome went wild with deafening cheers. The noise died down a bit moments later, though, when Puckett got tagged trying to steal third. The Twins, though, got a run in the sixth and another in the eighth to make the score 4-2.

The Cardinals had one more chance at bat. In the ninth inning, Puckett felt more nervous than he had ever been, even more than in his first game in the majors three years earlier. On his way out to center field, he told Gladden and Brunansky that he could literally hear his heart beating, even above the crowd noise. For the first and last time in his career, Puckett found himself silently pleading that the ball *not* be hit in his direction. "I was terrified I'd make the critical mistake," he later said. Naturally, the first batter hit a pop fly to short center field. Although it was not a tough catch,

Twins players celebrated after Kent Hrbek hit a grand slam in Game 6 of the 1987 World Series at the Metrodome in Minneapolis. The players were *(from left)* Hrbek, Greg Gagne, Kirby Puckett, and Don Baylor. Puckett scored four runs in Game 6, tying the record for runs scored in a single World Series game.

Puckett kept telling himself the whole time, "Please don't miss it! Please don't miss it." After he made the catch, he squeezed the ball with both hands and looked in his glove, just to make absolutely sure it was in there. Much to Puckett's relief, the next two outs went somewhere else. The game was over. The Minnesota Twins, the team no one expected to win, were the World Series champions.

Following the World Series win, the celebration in Minnesota should have been filled with excitement. For Puckett, however, it turned out to be a frightening experience. He and Tonya rode in a victory parade through downtown Minneapolis. Puckett sat in the back of the convertible with Tonya beside him. They were surrounded by what seemed like the entire city. That night, there was very little crowd control. Crazed fans lunged at the car. Puckett could hear people yell, "Grab her coat!" People threw toilet paper rolls, but not so they would unfurl and float down like confetti. Instead, they just tossed them hard at Kirby and Tonya. Fans also threw beer bottles, cans, and apples. It seemed more like a riot than a parade.

Kirby and Tonya were terrified. It took two hours for the cars to crawl through the downtown streets. For Puckett, it was like being an animal trapped in a cage. After that night, he refused to visit a zoo, because he had sympathy for the animals. Another parade in St. Paul went a lot more smoothly. Barricades were set up to keep people away from the cars. Plenty of police officers were on hand to control the crowds. Still, the experience opened Puckett's eyes to the new challenges life would bring as a World Series celebrity.

WITH THE VICTORY, THE AFTERSHOCK

After the World Series, life was never the same for Puckett in Minnesota. He could no longer enjoy quiet meals in restaurants or take strolls through shopping malls without being mobbed by fans. On one occasion, as recounted in his autobiography, a woman and her two children approached Puckett while he was Christmas shopping for his family at Toys "R" Us. The woman asked if he could sign an autograph for her kids. Puckett had his hands full, and he figured that, if he signed an autograph for one fan, he would suddenly have a line of people in front of him. He politely explained that he could not sign an autograph right then.

"You're serious?!" the woman screamed. "You mean you're not going to sign this?!"

"No, ma'am, I'm not," Puckett calmly replied. "I'm not signing anything. I'm Christmas shopping for my family, ma'am."

The woman yelled curses at him. Everyone in the store could hear her. When she finally realized that she was not getting an autograph, she grabbed her kids and stormed out of the store, screaming all the way. In the checkout line, other shoppers apologized for the woman's behavior and told Puckett that he had done the right thing. Nevertheless, Puckett did not go shopping much after that day.

People did not just bother Puckett in public. In later years, they came right up to his front door. Some were kids who maybe did not know any better. In these cases, Puckett politely explained that his home was the only place he could enjoy a private life. When adults came to the door, he was not as polite. "I don't sign at my own front door," Puckett said. "Sorry."

Some people found a somewhat legitimate way to get to Puckett's doorstep—Halloween. Parents would drive up his driveway, so he knew they were not the neighborhood kids. One year, a boy told Tonya that she had not given him enough candy. "We want more!" the boy shouted and pushed his way past Tonya into the house. As he grabbed another handful of candy from the bowl, his parents simply sat out in the car laughing.

For the most part, however, Puckett loved the fans. And they loved him back. Years later, when there was talk of Puckett's leaving the Twins for another team, fans worried that they might lose their favorite player. Manager Tom Kelly, though, had no such worries. He knew how much of Puckett's heart was with Minnesota—the team and the fans. When Puckett decided to sign another contract with the Twins, the local papers proclaimed, "The Puck Stops Here." Puckett had to agree, "I'm a Minnesota Twin forever."

The World Series aftermath was not all bad, however. Puckett got quite a bit of positive publicity, too. The Twins

Fans sought autographs from Kirby Puckett in August 2001 outside Doubleday Field at the Baseball Hall of Fame in Cooperstown, New York. The 1987 World Series victory thrust Puckett into the limelight in Minnesota. He and the fans loved one another—although sometimes people would invade Puckett's privacy to try to get an autograph from him at home.

released the Kirby Bear, a cuddly teddy bear. Puckett endorsed a pancake mix with a "great batter," and he went on a winter caravan promoting the Twins. Another huge plus came out of the World Series: a new contract, and this year at long last, Puckett was eligible for arbitration. He had finished 1987 hitting .332, with 28 homers, 32 doubles, and 5 triples. In the voting for Most Valuable Player, Puckett came in third behind George Bell of Toronto and Alan Trammell of Detroit. He was an All-Star player, and the Twins had won the World Series—both of which would increase his value.

Most important, Puckett wanted the Twins organization to be fair and pay him what he was worth. When a player goes to arbitration, he submits a figure and the club gives an offer. The arbitrator picks one or the other, nothing in between. Ron Shapiro and Puckett wanted to propose a number that was sufficient yet realistic, low enough that it might win the arbitration. At the same time, they wanted it high enough to get the Twins to negotiate a settlement, if possible. They came up with $1.35 million. The Twins, on the other hand, offered $930,000.

On the morning of arbitration, both groups gathered in a meeting room at an airport hotel. On one side of the table was Andy MacPhail, the Twins general manager; a representative from the Player Relations Department in the baseball commissioner's office; and Tal Smith, a consultant for the owners. On the opposite side sat Puckett, Shapiro, Mark Belanger from the Major League Baseball Players Association, and a couple of other lawyers. They had their coffee, juice, and muffins in front of them and were just about to get down to business when MacPhail looked across the table at Shapiro and asked, "Can we take a walk?"

They were gone for 45 minutes while the rest of the group nibbled on their breakfast and chatted about the weather. Then, Shapiro poked his head in the door and asked Puckett to join them in the lobby. Puckett sat down and got to hear a deal—$1,090,000 plus a bonus package worth $120,000. It was such a good offer that Puckett said at once, "Let's settle." Last-minute agreements like this one before arbitration are quite common. One reason it happened with Puckett was that the two numbers were far enough apart that somebody would end up a big winner and someone a big loser. If the Twins won, they feared it might affect Puckett's morale during the season. They did not want that.

Another World Series

Would the Twins be world champions again in 1988? That was the question everyone was asking. At the end of the season, the Twins had 91 wins, six more than in 1987. But the Oakland A's, their American League West rivals, sailed through the season with 104 wins. Kirby Puckett thought his Opening Day might have been a bad omen. Before the game, he was delayed watching the NCAA basketball championship and did not have time to shave his head. That day, he got his glove on a ball above the wall but could not hold onto it. The miss allowed a three-run homer for Mike Pagliarulo (who would later join the Twins in 1991). The Twins lost to the Yankees in a painful 8-0 decision. Being somewhat superstitious, Puckett thought that his unshaven head might have jinxed the very first game of the season, putting a damper on the rest of the year.

Individually, however, 1988 was Puckett's best year as a hitter up until that point. He had 24 homers, 121 RBIs, and became the fourth player ever to have 1,000 hits in his first five years in the majors. The other three were late greats Joe Medwick, Paul Waner, and Earle Combs. He also joined Rod Carew as the only other Twin to hit at least .300, have 200 hits, score 100 runs, and drive in 100 runs in the same season. That year, Puckett batted an impressive .356, the highest average by a right-handed hitter in the American League since Joe DiMaggio's .357 in 1941. Unfortunately, his average did not win him the batting title. Instead it went to Wade Boggs, who finished with an awesome .366. "When that happens," Puckett said in *I Love This Game!*, "you just tip your cap and wait till next year."

Puckett's average did earn him an unusual bonus. Before the season started, he played in a charity softball game held each February to benefit the battle against sickle-cell anemia. NBC covered the game, and announcer Bob Costas and Puckett had become friends over the years. That February, Costas's wife, Randy, was pregnant, and Puckett asked Costas what they were planning to name the baby. Costas said, "I'll tell you what. If you hit .350, we'll name our child Kirby." Obviously, Costas thought it was a long shot, because he had already promised to name the baby after Randy's brother Keith. Still, Costas kept up his end of the bargain, and named his son Keith Michael Kirby Costas.

In 1987 and 1988, the Twins earned a reputation in baseball as the blue-collar, hard-working team that functioned like a family. All of that changed in 1989. Frank Viola had won the Cy Young Award in 1988, after a brilliant season. He was 24–7 and basically unhittable. Afterward, a fight over his contract started. Viola and his agent turned down a $7.9 million deal for three years. Andy MacPhail gave up on talking to Viola's agent after the agent made some insulting public comments. Viola ended up accepting the contract anyway. By Opening Day, the situation between Viola and the Twins had soured the

Minnesota fans. Then, on Opening Day, he publicly announced that he would not be pitching for Minnesota the next season. Teammates and fans were shocked. That day, Viola went on to lose the game, and the fans booed him when Tom Kelly took him out in the seventh inning, with the bases loaded and nobody out. He lost his next four games, too, and the Twins lost 82 games altogether.

In July, as it became increasingly unlikely that the Twins would be in the pennant race, rumors spread about a Viola trade. He was eventually dealt to the New York Mets for five pitchers: Rick Aguilera, David West, Kevin Tapani, Jack Savage, and Tim Drummond.

A few weeks before the trade, Puckett played in the All-Star Game, voted in by the fans. Then, in a survey for *USA Today*, he was voted by the players and coaches as the best player in baseball. "Any player will tell you that being voted to the All-Star team by the fans is great," Puckett commented in his autobiography, "but extra recognition from other players is special because that has nothing to do with popularity and celebrity."

What excited Puckett even more than playing in the All-Star Game in Anaheim was meeting Willie Mays at Disneyland the Monday before the game. Mays was one of Puckett's childhood idols, along with baseball players like Ernie Banks and Billy Williams. Puckett thought Mays was the complete baseball player—he could run, hit, catch, steal, and more. Even at 29, Puckett still wanted to be like Mays, but he admitted that getting to that point would be tough, even for Kirby Puckett. Puckett figured he would fall short of Mays's career marks—660 home runs and 1,903 RBIs. At the get-together, Mays said he had been reading about Puckett. The two men shook hands and gave each other a hug.

By the end of 1989, the only excitement left for the Twins was Puckett's race for the batting title. Oddly, he had not been hitting the ball nearly as hard or as consistently as the previous year. Wade Boggs, though, was not having the best season

During a 1989 game against the Angels, Kirby Puckett connected for a hit. Puckett had his best hitting seasons in 1988 and 1989. In 1988, he hit an astounding .356 but lost the American League batting title to Wade Boggs. The following year, Puckett won the batting championship, with a .339 average.

either. Going into the final few games, he was about 10 points behind Puckett. In fact, Carney Lansford of the Oakland A's was Puckett's closest competitor. It all depended on how Puckett hit, and he was finishing up in Seattle at the Kingdome, where he never seemed to hit well.

In the first two games of the series, he was hitless, zero-for-seven. The batting title came down to the final game of the season. Puckett hit a double in the first inning. Then, he grounded out. During the game, the stadium was flashing Lansford's progress on the board. He was going hitless. At that point, Puckett could have sat down and won the title. In fact, Kelly asked him if he wanted to sit out the rest of the game. "You know I'm not like that, T.K.," Puckett said. His next time up to bat, he bounced a double off the right-center-field wall. While he was standing on second base, the stadium board flashed the announcement that Puckett had won the batting crown. The crowd answered with a standing ovation. His finished with an average of .339, while Lansford ended the season at .336.

During the winter before the 1989 season, the major leagues signed a $1 billion contract with CBS. Puckett had already signed a $2 million contract for 1989, avoiding arbitration and reaching that salary faster than any other ballplayer. Even though the Twins were considered a "small-market team," the speculation was that, after the 1989 season, Puckett would become baseball's first $3 million player. Interestingly, the Twins had a much lower budget than other major-league teams. Their local TV contracts paled in comparison with those of the New York teams—$50 million or more annually for the Yankees and Mets, $4 million for the Twins.

In 1990, Puckett would be eligible for free agency, in which his salary options could skyrocket. Andy MacPhail made it clear that he wanted to sign Puckett to a multiyear contract after the 1989 season, locking Puckett up before he became eligible for free agency. Puckett was fine with this plan, as long as the price was right. At first, the Twins offered $2.2 million or $2.3 million for each of three years. Puckett might have taken $2.4 million or $2.5 million, but the Twins would not budge. So negotiations dragged into the fall. At that point, the talks changed dramatically. By this time, Puckett had won the batting title, and other players had already signed for enormous sums. What originally looked outrageous in the spring would now have been considered a bargain for the Twins. Howard Johnson signed with the Mets for $6.9 million for three years, and Mike Scioscia signed with the Dodgers for $5.7 million for three years. Those players had not put up numbers as Puckett had year after year. "The discount days are over," Puckett commented.

As Tom Kelly put it, "Puck wants to play baseball, he wants to make money, and he wants to win." Puckett had to agree, but not in that order. He would have put money third. He did, however, want to earn the going wage. In the fall of 1989, the Twins finally offered $3 million annually, or $9 million for three years—the highest salary in the game. Puckett had to decide whether to take the money or wait to see what happened as a free agent. In the end, he decided that $3 million was a fair offer, and he signed. Just days later, other players signed bigger deals, but that was all right with Puckett. He was satisfied.

Not long after, Puckett's mother, Catherine, died on October 28. She had been in the hospital with heart trouble, but Puckett thought she would be getting out. "That was the hardest day of my life," Puckett said. Only 65 years old, she seemed too young to be gone. "A lot of people are more fortunate than I am," Puckett said. "But I was fortunate to have my mom with me for 29 years. So I can't complain."

Even at the $3 million mark, 1990 was not one of Puckett's best seasons. Near the end of the year, he was batting less than .300, but he still had a chance to reach that milestone with a good final series. The Twins finished up at the Metrodome against Seattle. Unfortunately, Puckett just missed his goal, with an average of .298.

Following the 1990 season, Kirby and Tonya adopted Catherine Margaret, after trying for four years to have a child of their own. They got the call one morning that she was born. In tears, Tonya woke Kirby up to tell him the news. A little later, the social worker brought over a picture of the baby. "[She] looked like the prettiest girl we'd ever seen, of course," Kirby later said in his autobiography. They found out that the baby would be coming home in five hours. Totally unprepared, they panicked. They rushed out to get diapers, blankets, and pink clothes. A new baby Puckett was a wonderful way to bring out a new beginning in Kirby for the 1991 season. Two years later, they adopted a little boy—Kirby, Jr., of course.

FROM LAST TO FIRST

The 1991 season began rather strangely for Puckett. It all started late in 1990, when the Twins were going nowhere as a team, and Puckett told Tom Kelly that maybe he could play right field. The Twins had four good outfielders—Dan Gladden, Shane Mack, Puckett, and a new player, Pedro Muñoz. Puckett thought he had slowed down a step or two in the past seven years. He would turn 31 during spring training in 1991. Right field did not require as much running as center field. For pure speed and natural ability, Puckett believed Mack was now the best defensive player in the outfield.

A center fielder is always on the move. If a player hits the ball to shortstop, a center fielder has to run behind there to cover in case the shortstop misses the ball. Likewise, if a ball goes to second, the center fielder has to cover behind the base. If a guy is stealing second base, the center fielder has to run to back that up. Plus, the pitcher's mound is a major hazard for the center fielder's throw home. The throw to home plate has to clear the pitcher's mound, either in the air or on the first bounce. In right or left field, it is a straight throw to home. All in all, it is a little easier to play right or left field.

Puckett felt the team was better off with Mack at center. So he told Tom Kelly that, if he agreed, they could give it a try. One afternoon in Cleveland, not long after, Puckett glanced at the lineup on the board. There his name was, batting third of course, but with the number 9 (right field) next to his name. Although he could have used a little more warning, he did fine in right field that day. For the rest of the 1990 season, Kelly experimented with switching the outfielders around.

During spring training in 1991, Puckett was playing a lot in right field. When Kelly asked him how he felt out there, Puckett said, "Great." He truly meant it, too, and thought the move was a good one. On Opening Day in Oakland, Puckett started in right field. In the fourth inning, with runners on first and second, an Oakland batter lofted a fly ball into foul territory down the right-field line. Puckett ran over to glove the ball. It was a catchable ball, nothing tricky, but the ball hit the heel of Puckett's glove and dropped out. Puckett knew it was his fault. That catch would have been the third out and the end of the inning. Instead, the batter hit a three-run homer on the next pitch. The Twins lost, 7-2. Puckett's error, more or less, cost them the game.

Puckett's Opening Day fumble turned out to be his only mistake over the next couple of weeks playing right field. To Puckett, it seemed as if everyone was comfortable in his new position. Then, one day, Kelly walked up to Puckett in the clubhouse. "Let me talk to you for a minute, Puck," he said, according to *I Love This Game!*

"Yeah, T, what's up?" Puckett replied.

"That's it for the experiment," Kelly said.

"Why?" Puckett asked, somewhat shocked.

"Just tell me where you want to play," Kelly said.

"Well, I'm having fun in right field," Puckett started. "I've played center most of my life so I wouldn't say I *don't* want to play center—"

Kelly interrupted him, "Where do you *want* to play?"

Puckett thought it over for a moment. "Well," he said, "center field."

"That's where you play then," Kelly decided. He was tired of toying around with the situation and wanted it settled. The next game, Puckett was back in center field, and he stayed there for the rest of 1991.

The experts were dead wrong to pick the Twins to finish low in 1991. They were right, however, about April. Historically, the Twins play poorly in April, and 1991 was no exception, with the Twins achieving a 9–11 record. Still, they were wrong about the rest of the season, for two reasons. First, the Twins were not a bad team in 1990, despite their lousy record. Second, they made many improvements during the off-season.

Puckett, on the other hand, was not feeling so good about his hitting. Despite a .319 average for the season, higher than in 1990, he felt that this season was his toughest hitting year. "I just never saw the ball real well in 1991," Puckett later said in his autobiography. "I had one hot streak in July—hot according to the numbers—but I never felt I carried the Twins, not for a single week. Your No. 3 hitter should do that every so often." Once again, Puckett found himself examining the videos and spending more time than he ever had in "the hole"—the batting-cage area down the right-field line in the Metrodome. He took extra batting practice, then more batting practice. He worked on keeping his shoulder in, holding his head still, and timing his high leg kick. Still, he felt out of sync. Kent Hrbek often teased Puckett about coming to the plate just after Puckett had hit a pitch that was three feet outside the plate and ripped it for a single. "How did Puckett ever hit that pitch?" the opposing catcher would grumble.

Minnesota Twins fans do a wave of a different sort—a wave of their Homer Hankies, in a game in September 1991. The white handkerchief with the red logo became popular during the Twins' World Series run in 1987 and again during their trip into the postseason in 1991.

When he was seeing the ball, that kind of free swinging was incredible. In 1991, though, Puckett doubted that Hrbek heard much complaining from the catchers.

Even still, the Twins came up from last place to first. At the end of the season, they had won the division with a 95–67 record. Once again, the Twins were headed to the American League Championship Series, this time facing the best of the East—the Toronto Blue Jays. In the playoffs, the Twins beat the Blue Jays in five games, winning the last three in Toronto to everyone's surprise. As in 1987, Puckett started out the series slowly, one-for-seven in the first two games. Luckily, he caught fire in the next three games—hitting eight-for-fourteen, with two homers and four RBIs. He was named the Most Valuable Player of the championship series.

For the second time in five years, the Minnesota Twins were going to the World Series. Meanwhile, the Twins awaited the winner of the National League Championship Series between the Pittsburgh Pirates and the Atlanta Braves. The series ran seven games, and when the Braves beat Pittsburgh in the final game, it set up one of the strangest World Series baseball had ever seen. Both teams had finished last in their division the year before. Now the Twins and the Braves were pitted against each other in the World Series. But there was much more in store.

☆☆☆☆☆☆

THE HOMER HANKY

During the 1987 pennant race, the Minneapolis/St. Paul newspaper the *Star Tribune* transformed a common handkerchief into a baseball-cheering phenomenon. It created the Official Star Tribune Minnesota Twins Homer Hanky, or "Homer Hanky," as it is simply called. A red, baseball-shaped logo was printed on a white handkerchief and sold to fans. When cheering the Twins, Minnesota fans would frantically wave their Homer Hankies. During the Twins' championship seasons in 1987 and 1991, the stands often resembled a sea of bobbing whitecaps.

A new Homer Hanky was printed for the 2006 season, when the Twins once again battled back from a losing record to make it to the American League Division Series. Fans wondered if the Twins would make it to another World Series—one more for the Puck. Unfortunately, the season ended when they lost to the Oakland A's in a three-game sweep.

WORLD SERIES NO. 2

People have called the 1991 World Series the greatest in history. It featured five nail-biting, one-run games, three of which went into extra innings. Four games were decided in the very last at-bat. The final game stretched on for an excruciating 10 innings.

The World Series started routinely in Minnesota at the Metrodome. The Twins won, 5-2, spurred by Gagne's three-run homer and a single shot by Hrbek. As usual, Puckett started out dragging, going hitless in four trips to the plate. In Game 2, things got interesting. At the top of the third inning, Minnesota was up, 2-1. Atlanta's Lonnie Smith reached first on an error by Twins rookie third baseman Scott Leius. Next, Atlanta's Ron Gant hit a single to left, and a bad throw by left fielder Dan Gladden skipped past Leius. Gant rounded first, heading for second. Pitcher Kevin Tapani grabbed the ball and fired it to Hrbek at first, hoping to nab Gant as he dove back to first.

What happened next has become a piece of World Series lore. As the 170-pound (77-kilogram) Gant lunged back to the bag, the 250-pound (113-kilogram) Hrbek seemingly lifted Gant off the bag and tagged him. The umpire called him out, the Braves were stunned, and the Metrodome shook with excited tension.

Hrbek defended himself. "His momentum carried him into me," he said. "I knew he was going to fall off the bag because that's where his momentum was taking him."

Enraged, Gant rebutted, "I don't know since when you can just pull a guy off the bag."

In any case, the Twins took the game, 3-2, putting them ahead two games to none in the World Series. Game 3 took the teams to Atlanta's Fulton County Stadium, where the fans were not forgiving of Hrbek's stunt. Feelings were so bitter that Hrbek even received a death threat. Before the game, Puckett pulled Hrbek aside and asked, "Now, you're not going to act the fool out there, are you?" Naturally, Puckett cared about the behavior of his friend and teammate. He also would be standing next to Hrbek during the introduction. If Braves fans started chucking objects at Hrbek, Puckett would be in the line of fire.

"Take it easy, Herbie, please," Puckett begged.

"Okay, okay," Hrbek promised.

As soon as Hrbek stepped onto the field, the boos started raining down from the stands. Instead of ignoring them, Hrbek egged the fans on. Luckily, the situation did not get out of hand. The next three games, however, belonged to the Braves, even though Puckett managed to get a couple of hits, including one home run. Game 6 would be back at the Metrodome. The Twins would need a win at home, or they would lose the World Series.

Before Game 6, Puckett walked into the clubhouse at the Metrodome. All the guys seemed serious and quiet, too quiet. "Hey, this is the World Series," Puckett thought. "It's a privilege to play in the World Series, not a chore." Puckett decided that his teammates needed to loosen up. He spread a little extra enthusiasm that day, going from guy to guy, pepping them up. Then, he suddenly shouted, "Jump on board, boys! I'm going to carry us tonight. Don't even worry about it. Just back me up a little bit, and I'll take us to Game 7." A little bold, perhaps, but Puckett had a good feeling about that game.

Game 6 was the game that won Puckett tremendous fame in the 1991 World Series. With the score tied, 3-3, in the eleventh inning, Puckett hit his famous home run to win the game. He made a promise, and he delivered. With the World Series tied, everything came down to Game 7.

The deciding game on October 27 was another nail-biter. For nine innings, the Twins and the Braves held each other to a scoreless tie, the first scoreless game to go to extra innings in World Series history. In the bottom of the tenth, with the

After hitting the winning home run in Game 6 of the 1991 World Series, Kirby Puckett was mobbed by his teammates. The Minnesota Twins went on to beat the Atlanta Braves in Game 7 to capture the championship.

bases loaded, Twins pinch hitter Gene Larkin put an end to the hair-raising World Series with a pop fly over the heads of the drawn in Braves' outfielders. Dan Gladden came home to score the run that clinched a second World Series for Kirby Puckett and the Minnesota Twins.

Although Puckett's star performance in Game 6 brought him overnight recognition, he does not single that game out as his main memory of the 1991 World Series. Instead, he simply said, "We won, man, we won. That's all I know."

TRAILING YEARS

As it turned out, 1991 was the pinnacle for Puckett and the Twins. In the years after the World Series, the team just did not have enough to get back on top. Puckett, however, continued to throw his best into the game. In 1992, he started off smoking, with a .374 batting average, seven home runs, and 25 RBIs in May. That month, he had an astounding .636 slugging percentage and had his first grand slam home run, after 5,193 at-bats and 131 career homers. Five days later, he got his second grand slam. He was named the American League Player of the Month in May, and again the following month. In June, Puckett had a .336 batting average, 5 more home runs, and 24 RBIs. He was only the second player to earn the honor two months in a row. New York Yankee Don Mattingly had also done it in 1985. In August, he hit his third grand slam. Puckett finished the season with a .329 average, 19 home runs, and 110 RBIs. He placed second to Oakland's Dennis Eckersley as the American League Most Valuable Player.

Puckett's contract was up after the 1992 season. Other teams, like the Boston Red Sox and the Philadelphia Phillies, pursued him, and Puckett visited those cities. In the end, though, he decided to remain a Twin, signing a five-year, $30 million contract in December, even though he could have received more money from other teams.

In 1993, Puckett earned his eighth straight trip to the All-Star Game, this time winning the game's MVP award with a home run and an RBI double in an American League victory. Still, his overall stats for the season dipped to his lowest in years, with a .296 batting average, 22 home runs, and 89 RBIs. For most players, these numbers would make for an awesome season. For Puckett, they were below his standards.

Puckett made a tremendous comeback in 1994. In April, he set a club record with 26 RBIs. He was averaging .317, with 20 home runs and 112 RBIs, when a baseball strike cut

Kirby Puckett gets a handshake from Third Base Coach Sparky Anderson after hitting a home run in the 1993 All-Star Game. Puckett was named the Most Valuable Player of the game. His season batting average, though, fell to .296 in 1993.

the year short in mid-August. Once the strike was settled and play resumed in 1995, Puckett's career changed. His playing time at center field was drastically cut. More often, he played in right and left field, or as a designated hitter. Nevertheless, he posted solid numbers, a .314 average, 23 home runs, and 99 RBIs.

In the few short seconds it takes for a fastball to reach home plate, Puckett's electrifying career came to a screeching halt. One tragic injury would give way to an earth-shattering discovery. On September 28, 1995, in a meaningless game late in the season, Cleveland Indians pitcher Dennis Martínez fired a fastball that struck Puckett in the face. It was a pivotal moment in the history of the Minnesota Twins and the life of Kirby Puckett.

After the Lights Go Out

Throughout his baseball career, Kirby Puckett had conquered thousands of fastballs. But on that September afternoon at the Metrodome, in front of barely 9,000 fans, a fastball got the best of Puckett. In the first inning of a game that would turn out to be a 12-4 win for the Indians, Puckett took his spot in the batter's box. Indians starter Dennis Martínez, who was a good friend of Puckett's, had a reputation for throwing inside. This time, he did it to Puckett. On a 1-2 count, Martínez sailed a fastball high and tight, and Puckett just could not get out of the way quickly enough. The ball struck Puckett's face with a painful smack. Puckett dropped to the ground, a pool of blood forming next to him.

Getting hit in the head by a pitch is a baseball player's worst nightmare. The injury itself can be devastating, but

often, the emotional scars can run deeper. Players who never before thought twice about stepping up to a 90-mile-per-hour (145-kilometer-per-hour) pitch suddenly know the dangers. A ballplayer can become so intimidated that he may never play again.

At the moment, however, these thoughts were far from anyone's mind. The most popular player in Twins history was twisting in agony on the ground. Fortunately, the damage was not as bad as it could have been. Puckett did not need surgery, but the injury was still severe. He had a fractured left upper jawbone, two knocked-out teeth, and several lacerations in his mouth.

The incident mortified Martínez. "It was the worst feeling I have ever had in my lifetime," he said. "I almost took myself out after that inning. I understand how the fans feel. . . . He's one of my best friends." The next day, Puckett exonerated Martínez. "I know he didn't mean to hit me," Puckett said. "His ball just moves so much. Dennis is a good friend of mine, and I know it wasn't intentional."

To Puckett, the injury was only a minor setback. He figured that, after a few weeks of rest and the off-season, he would be as good as new and ready for the 1996 season. At first, it seemed as if it was going to happen that way. His jaw healed, and six months later he was at spring training. There were no mental scars to be found. "It takes more than a 90-mile-an-hour fastball to make me change," Puckett claimed.

On March 27, 1996, Puckett stepped up to the plate in a game during spring training. True to form, he hammered a pitch 450 feet (137 meters) to dead center. Two innings later, he hit another ball way out to left center. The old "Puck" was back.

The next morning, however, Puckett woke up with a black dot in the middle of his right eye. He told Tonya that he could not see her. As strange as it was, Puckett did not give it much thought. He just assumed he had slept on his eye wrong and it would go away. Upon examination, doctors diagnosed Puckett with glaucoma, a group of diseases that damage the optic nerve. If left untreated, glaucoma can cause blindness. Initially, doctors were hopeful that they could treat Puckett's glaucoma and correct his blurry vision. They suspected there was blockage in one of the veins that drained blood from the retina. More than likely, he would be ready to play in two weeks, six weeks at the most. Puckett visited a retinal specialist at Johns Hopkins University in Baltimore, Maryland. There, doctors drained some fluid from his eye, gave him some medication, and told him to wait for it to heal.

A few days later, Puckett was back in the Twins dugout at the Metrodome for Opening Day against the Detroit Tigers. This time, Puckett would not be playing. It must have been tough for Puckett to sit that game out, but he was optimistic that he would quickly heal. "This eye's got a thunderstorm, and it's cloudy," Puckett said as he tapped his patched right eye. "And this one's bright and sunny." He pointed to his left eye. "I've just got two different shades. But it feels fine."

As much as the Twins and their fans wanted to see Puckett back on the field, everyone was more concerned about his health. "You don't even worry about the baseball part of things right now with Puck," manager Tom Kelly said. "When you're talking about your eyesight, the game is irrelevant. On a zero-to-10 scale, baseball is a zero."

Still, without Puckett on the field, it just did not seem like Twins baseball. Even the opposing teams missed seeing him out there. "I can't remember playing a game against the Twins and Kirby not being a part of it," said Baltimore's All-Star shortstop Cal Ripken, Jr. "It just doesn't seem right coming in here and him not being here."

All the optimism in the world would not make Puckett's condition go away. Every morning when Puckett woke up, he would open his right eye first to find out if he could

During a news conference to announce his retirement in July 1996, Kirby Puckett waved to some of his teammates. With Puckett was his wife, Tonya. Puckett announced his retirement just hours after undergoing surgery for glaucoma that revealed irreversible damage to the retina of his eye.

see clearly. Morning after morning passed, with no change. In the meantime, Puckett hung out in the clubhouse and dressed in his uniform for every game, hoping for the day he could play again.

Puckett went to the best eye doctors in the country. He made another trip to Baltimore and then two trips to the prestigious Mayo Clinic in Rochester, Minnesota, for a second opinion. Sometimes laser surgery can help glaucoma. Puckett underwent three surgeries, with no improvement. Finally on July 12, in a last-ditch effort, Puckett had a vitrectomy. The surgery, though, was unsuccessful. It only confirmed what the doctors had suspected and what baseball fans feared— Puckett would not recover. His baseball career was over. The hit that Puckett suffered late in the 1995 season had nothing to do with the problem in his right eye. The disease was simply hereditary—William Puckett also had glaucoma. Eventually, Puckett would go completely blind in his right eye.

After receiving the crushing news, Puckett was unbelievably strong. "I was prepared," he said. "I mean, there's no way you can be prepared for this, but I was prepared for life after baseball."

Shortly after, he held a press conference announcing his retirement from baseball at the age of 36. Puckett did not have a speech prepared. He simply spoke from his heart. "Now it is time for me to close the chapter in this book on baseball and go on to another part of my life," he said. "Kirby Puckett is going to be all right. Don't worry about me. I will show up, but I am going to have fun and have a smile on my face. The only thing is that I won't have this uniform on. But you guys have a lot of memories of what I did when I did have it on."

After 12 seasons with the Minnesota Twins, the stadium lights went out on Puckett's career, and he said his final farewell to baseball. He ended his career with 2,304 hits. If he had been able to play the three to four more years he planned, he probably would have reached that magical 3,000-hit mark. During his years in the majors, he had 207 home runs, drove in 1,085 runs, scored 1,071 runs, and finished with a career batting average of .318, the highest career average for a right-handed batter since Joe DiMaggio at that point. He won six Gold Gloves and was named to 10 straight All-Star Games.

In 1997, the Minnesota Twins retired his uniform number, 34. Four years later, Puckett was elected to the National

The 2001 inductees into the Baseball Hall of Fame saluted the fans during a ceremony in August of that year in Cooperstown, New York. The inductees were *(from left)* Bill Mazeroski, Dave Winfield, and Kirby Puckett.

Baseball Hall of Fame in his first year of eligibility. "There may be a few people out there who remember a time when the word on Kirby Puckett was that he was too short or didn't have the power to make it to the big leagues," Puckett said during the induction ceremony at the Hall of Fame in 2001. "Well, despite the fact that I didn't get to play all the years I wanted to, I did it. And to any young person out there . . . I want you to remember the guiding principles of my life: You can be what you want to be, if you believe in yourself and you work hard, because anything, and I'm telling you, anything, is possible."

CONTROVERSY AND TRAGEDY

The years following Puckett's retirement from baseball were marred with controversy. Increasingly, his private life seemed to contradict his much revered public image. Some people close to him felt that, after he could no longer play baseball, he became conceited and abusive. His weight ballooned to 300 pounds (136 kilograms). In 2002, Kirby and Tonya got a divorce after Tonya allegedly caught him having an intimate phone call with another woman. She hired a private investigator and

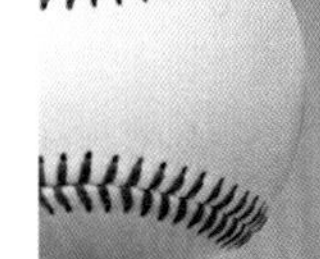

BEGINNINGS OF THE BASEBALL HALL OF FAME

On June 12, 1939, 15,000 visitors flooded Main Street in Cooperstown, New York. There, they listened to baseball legend Babe Ruth give his acceptance speech as one of the first 26 Hall of Famers. Shortly after noon, the museum opened its doors to the public. June 12 was the crowning day of a four-month celebration of the 100th anniversary of baseball in Cooperstown—the home of baseball.

The two-story, Colonial-style building took three years to construct. James River Colonial brick was used on the walls, topped with a slate roof. Five identical windows lined the front of the second story, where a baseball flag flapped in the breeze. Majestic pillars stood boldly at the entrance. Four white marble steps framed with wrought-iron railings led up to the doorway. In the wall out front, the white granite keystone had been carved with a baseball design.

At the grand opening, the Hall of Fame was a 1,200-square-foot room that served as a gallery, a museum, a library, a ticket office, a retail shop, and a director's office. The second floor was used to store library materials. This first museum was humble

found out that Kirby was having an affair. "In the beginning, I was absolutely devastated," Tonya Puckett said. "I loved him so much. I was one of those people who didn't think I could live without him. It's like you're in this tunnel and it's so dark and you can't see. And one day you wake up and you see light. You keep following this light." She even claimed that Puckett had abused her at times during their marriage and had one time threatened to kill her. Although Tonya said she never wanted her statements to go public, the news seeped out. Kirby denied

☆☆☆☆☆☆

compared with today's three-story, state-of-the-art masterpiece. Years later, the first floor became the Cooperstown Room. Still later, it held the Perez-Steele Art Gallery.

In 1939, visitors walked beneath a grand chandelier and paused for a moment in front of a fireplace. There, they looked at the famous Doubleday baseball perched in a glass case on the mantle. Above the fireplace hung an oil painting of Abner Doubleday, the Civil War general who contributed to the start of baseball in Cooperstown. Throughout the gallery, dozens of cases held numerous baseball artifacts—including a baseball from Cy Young's 500th win in 1910. There were also uniforms from great players and, of course, the 26 plaques of the first Hall of Famers. These Hall of Famers included the first five elected in 1936—Babe Ruth, Ty Cobb, Walter Johnson, Christy Mathewson, and Honus Wagner—as well as those elected in 1937, 1938, and 1939.

Today, the enormous facility displays thousands of artifacts, photos, paintings, and other baseball souvenirs—such as Rickey Henderson's spikes, Pete Rose's bat, Hank Aaron's 700th home run baseball, and Reggie Jackson's Angels helmet.

Tonya's accusations, but the damage had been done. Suddenly, the man who had been voted Baseball's Best Role Model and Friendliest Player in 1993 had a tarnished reputation.

People wondered if Kirby Puckett was really the man they thought he was. It was reported that he performed lewd acts in public, such as an incident in which he allegedly urinated in plain view at a shopping mall parking lot. On September 5, 2002, in Edina, Minnesota, he was arrested and charged with supposedly pulling a woman into a bar restroom and groping her. He denied the charges and was later tried and acquitted. In the winter of 2003, Puckett moved to Scottsdale, Arizona, perhaps because of the mounting controversy in Minnesota. A few years later, he became engaged to Jodi Olson, and the two of them planned to be married on June 24, 2006. Puckett, however, would never walk down the aisle a second time.

On March 5, 2006, Puckett suffered a massive hemorrhagic stroke at his home in Scottsdale. He was rushed to Scottsdale Osborn Hospital. That same day, doctors performed neurosurgery to relieve the pressure on his brain. Sadly, the surgery failed, and he was transferred to St. Joseph's Hospital and Medical Center in Phoenix on life support. His former teammates and coaches were notified the following morning. Many of them flew to Phoenix to be at his bedside during his final hours, including 1991 teammates Shane Mack and Kent Hrbek. Also there were his fiancée Jodi, his former wife, Tonya, and their two children, Catherine and Kirby, Jr. Puckett died on March 6, shortly after being disconnected from life support, just eight days shy of his forty-sixth birthday. Behind Lou Gehrig, Puckett was the second-youngest Hall of Famer (inducted while living) to die.

Baseball fans across the country mourned the death of a great player. For Minnesota fans, it was like losing a close friend. Thousands of Twins fans stacked stuffed animals and good-bye letters outside the Metrodome as a memorial to him.

Fans filled the seats of the Metrodome on March 12, 2006, for a memorial service for Kirby Puckett. He died on March 6, just eight days shy of his forty-sixth birthday, after suffering a stroke at his home in Scottsdale, Arizona.

On the afternoon of March 12 (declared "Kirby Puckett Memorial Day" in Minneapolis), a private memorial service was held in the Twin Cities suburb of Wayzata. Later, a public ceremony was held at the Metrodome—attended by family, friends, ballplayers past and present, and about 15,000 fans. A sellout crowd was predicted, but an incoming blizzard that night kept many from attending. Before the service, from 5:00 to 7:00 P.M., volunteers rang bells playing "We're Gonna Win Twins" and "Take Me Out to the Ball Game," Inside the

Metrodome, a sea of flowers surrounded a huge No. 34 banner in the middle of the ball field. Puckett jerseys dotted the stands, proudly worn by tear-filled fans. "Make sure you smile and laugh tonight because that's what Kirby would want, and that's why we love him," said Twins radio announcer John Gordon in his introductory remarks.

As Kirby Puckett would have wanted, the night was less about crying and moments of silence and more about celebrating his life. The brightest cheers came during two video tributes and former public-address announcer Bob Casey's famed introduction, "Kir-beeeee Puck-ett!" The people in the crowd roared again as they relived Puckett's amazing performance in Game 6 of the 1991 World Series. As the video clip of his famous home run played, fans once again waved their Homer Hankies.

Hall of Famers Harmon Killebrew and Dave Winfield also spoke at the memorial service, as did a multitude of former teammates and coaches. "I'm not going to remember the hits and the hustle and the catches that Kirby made, because I think it's going to happen again by different people," said Hrbek, the former Twins first baseman and longtime teammate of Puckett's. "I'm going to remember the smile, I'm going to remember the laughter, I'm going to remember the clubhouse pranks, and just having a good ol' time with Puck."

In honor of Puckett, Twins players wore a black "34" on the right sleeves of their uniforms for the 2006 season. The team also painted Puckett's number on the Metrodome turf, one between home plate and first base and another between third and home. Baseball fans remember Puckett as a Hall of Famer, an All-Star center fielder, and a hard hitter. In Minnesota, fans will remember Kirby Puckett as the greatest Twins player of all time.

STATISTICS

KIRBY PUCKETT

Primary position: Center field (Also RF, LF)

Full name: Kirby Puckett • Born: March 14, 1960, Chicago, Illinois • Died: March 6, 2006, Phoenix, Arizona • Height: 5'8" • Weight: 210 lbs. • Team: Minnesota Twins (1984–1995)

YEAR	TEAM	G	AB	H	HR	RBI	BA
1984	MIN	128	557	165	0	31	.296
1985	MIN	161	691	199	4	74	.288
1986	MIN	161	680	223	31	96	.328
1987	MIN	157	624	207	28	99	.332
1988	MIN	158	657	234	24	121	.356
1989	MIN	159	635	215	9	85	.339
1990	MIN	146	551	164	12	80	.298
1991	MIN	152	611	195	15	89	.319
1992	MIN	160	639	210	19	110	.329
1993	MIN	156	622	184	22	89	.296
1994	MIN	108	439	139	20	112	.317
1995	MIN	137	538	169	23	99	.314
TOTALS		1,783	7,244	2,304	207	1,085	.318

Key: MIN = Minnesota Twins; G = Games; AB = At-bats; H = Hits; HR = Home runs; RBI = Runs batted in; BA = Batting average

CHRONOLOGY

1960 **March 14** Born in Chicago, Illinois, to William and Catherine Puckett.

1982 **January 12** Is the Twins' first pick (third overall) in baseball's secondary draft.

June 23 Makes minor-league debut with Elizabethton in the Appalachian League.

1984 **May 8** Is called up to the major leagues by the Twins; becomes the ninth player in big-league history to get four hits (4-for-5) in his first game.

1985 **April 22** Hits his first major-league home run.

1986 Plays in his first All-Star Game.

November 1 Marries Tonya Hudson.

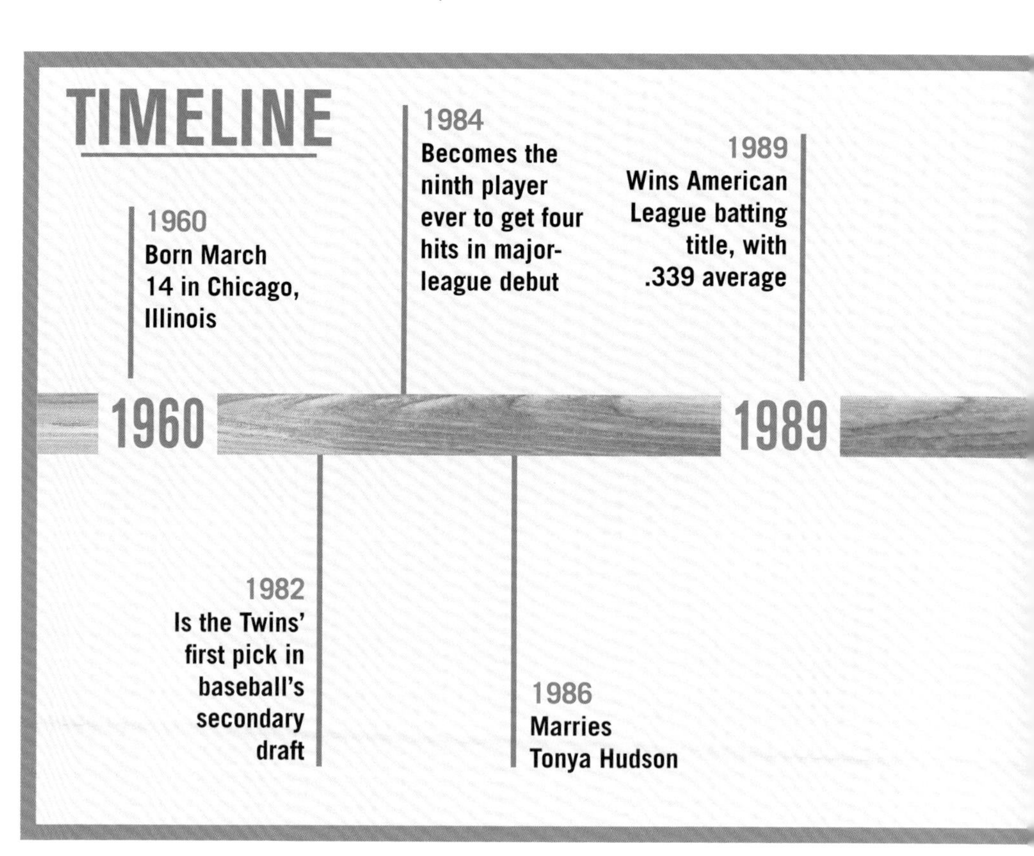

1987 **August 30** Ties the American League record for hits (six) in a nine-inning game, sets club record for total bases (14), and ties team mark for extra-base hits (four) in a game; sets the American League record and ties the major-league record for hits (10) in two consecutive games.

Twins win the World Series.

1988 Becomes the fourth player in baseball history to reach 1,000 hits in first five seasons.

1989 Finishes season with .339 batting average, winning the American League batting title.

1990 **May 12** Hits 100th career home run.

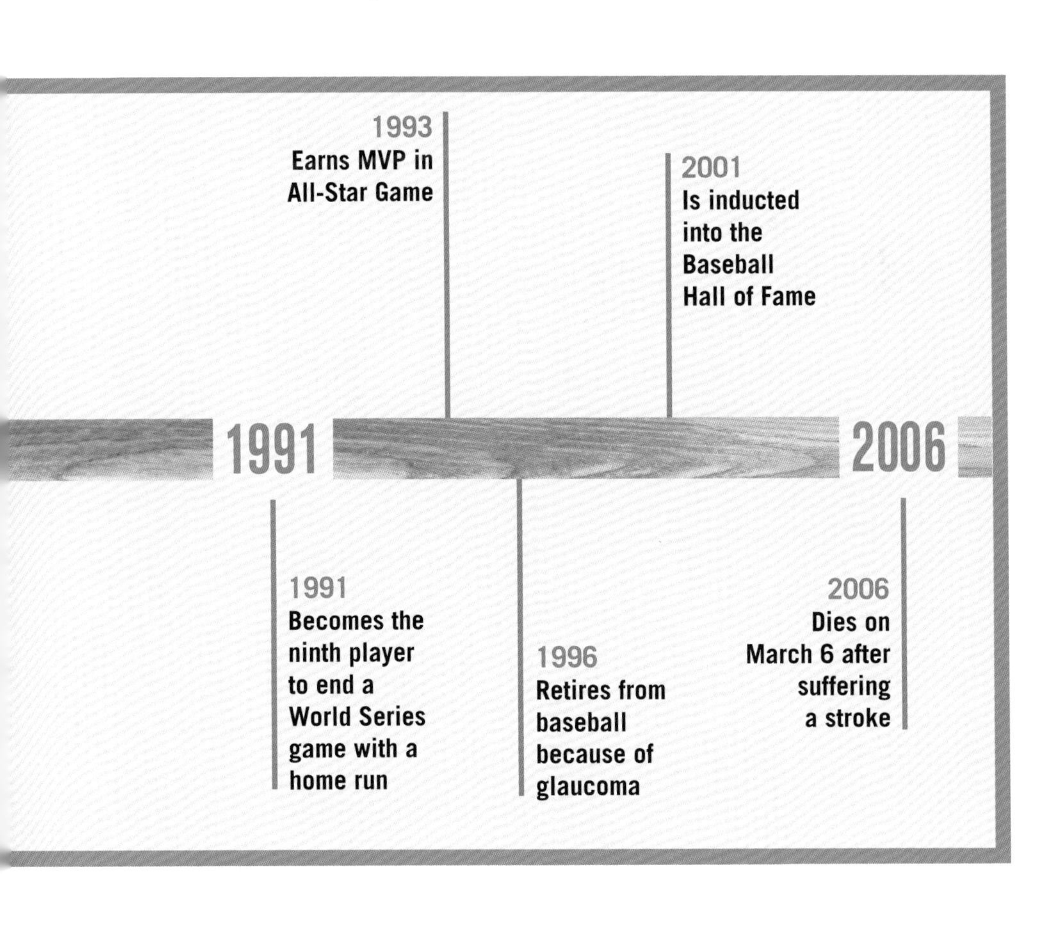

1991 **October 13** Named the Most Valuable Player of the American League Championship Series after going 9-for-21 with two home runs and six RBIs.

October 26 Becomes the ninth player to end a World Series game with a home run.

1993 **July 13** Earns MVP award in the All-Star Game—his eighth consecutive appearance in the Midsummer Classic.

1994 **June 26** Becomes Twins' all-time hits leader (2,086).

1995 **September 28** Is hit on the left side of his face by a pitch and fractures his jawbone.

1996 **March 28** Wakes up with blurred vision, four days before start of the season.

March 29 Placed on the disabled list for the first time in career.

July 12 Announces retirement from baseball because of glaucoma.

2001 **August 5** Is inducted into the Baseball Hall of Fame.

2002 Wife Tonya files for divorce, alleging that Puckett abused her and threatened to kill her.

September 5 Is charged with sexually assaulting a woman in the restroom of a bar.

2003 **April 3** Is acquitted of the sexual-assault charges.

2006 **March 5** Suffers a stroke at his home in Scottsdale, Arizona, and dies the next day, March 6.

GLOSSARY

arbitration The process by which a third party settles a salary dispute between a player and a team. In baseball, the player and the team each submit a salary figure to the arbitrator. The arbitrator then picks one or the other; there is no compromise.

assist The official scorer awards an assist to every defensive player who fields or touches the ball (after it is hit by the batter) before a putout.

at-bat (AB) An official turn at batting that is charged to a baseball player, except when the player walks, sacrifices, is hit by a pitched ball, or is interfered with by a catcher. At-bats are used to calculate a player's batting average and slugging percentage.

batting average The average number of hits per at-bat (batting average equals hits divided by at-bats); a batting average of .300 is considered excellent.

bunt A ball not fully hit, with the batter intending to get to first base before the infielder can throw him out, or allowing an existing base runner to advance a base.

cellar Last place in the standings.

curveball A pitch that curves on its way to the plate, thanks to the spin a pitcher places on the ball when throwing. Also know as a "breaking ball."

designated hitter In the American League, a player who bats each time for the pitcher. There is no designated hitter in the National League. Baseball is the only professional sport in which different rules apply in different sections of the league. The lack of consistency about the designated hitter is an ongoing debate.

doubleheader Two games played by the same two teams on the same day.

error The game's scorer designates an error when a defensive player makes a mistake that results in a runner reaching base, or advancing to a base.

fastball A pitch that is thrown more for high velocity than for movement; it is the most common type of pitch.

knuckleball A pitch thrown without spin—traditionally thrown with the knuckles but also with the fingertips. It generally flutters and moves suddenly on its way to the plate.

leadoff hitter The first batter listed on a team's lineup card.

on deck The offensive player next in line to bat is said to be on deck. Often the player on deck will swing a weighted bat to warm up and stay in an area called the on-deck circle.

runs batted in (RBI) The number of runs that score as a direct result of a batter's hit(s) are the runs batted in by that batter. The major-league record is 191 RBIs for a single season by one batter.

slider A relatively fast pitch with a slight curve in the opposite direction of the throwing arm.

slugging percentage The number of bases a player reaches divided by the number of at-bats. It is a measure of the power of a batter.

strike zone The area directly over home plate up to the batter's chest (roughly where the batter's uniform lettering is) and down to his or her knees. Different umpires have slightly different strike zones, and players only ask that they be consistent.

total bases The sum of all the bases a hitter has accumulated. A single = 1; a double = 2; a triple = 3; a home run = 4.

BIBLIOGRAPHY

Carlson, Chuck. *Kirby Puckett: Baseball's Last Warrior.* Lenexa, Kans.: Addax Publishing Group, 1997.

Goldstein, Richard. "Kirby Puckett, 45, Hall of Fame Outfielder, Dies." *New York Times*, March 7, 2006.

Puckett, Kirby. *I Love This Game!: My Life and Baseball.* New York: HarperCollins Publishers, 1993.

Puckett, Kirby, and Greg Brown. *Be the Best You Can Be.* Minneapolis, Minn.: Waldman House Press, 1993.

Sansevere, Bob. "The Secret Life of Kirby Puckett." *St. Paul Pioneer Press*, December 17, 2002.

WCCO.com. "Fans, Friends Remember Puckett." Available online at *http://wcco.com/sports/local_story_071120850.html.* March 13, 2006.

———. "Fans Mourn Puckett at Metrodome Memorial." Available online at *http://wcco.com/sports/local_story_066143658.html.* March 8, 2006.

———. "Kirby Puckett Memorial Day Proclaimed." Available online at *http://wcco.com/sports/local_story_070175522.html.* March 12, 2006.

———. "Twins Great Kirby Puckett Dies." Available online at *http://wcco.com/sports/local_story_065104727.html.* March 7, 2006.

———. "Twins Tribute Puckett With '34' Patches." Available online at *http://www.WCCO.com/sports/local_story_075085033.html.* March 16, 2006.

FURTHER READING

Carlson, Chuck. *Kirby Puckett: Baseball's Last Warrior.* Lenexa, Kans.: Addax Publishing Group, 1997.

Hrbek, Kent, with Dennis Brackin. *Kent Hrbek's Tales From the Minnesota Twins Dugout.* Champaign, Ill.: Sports Publishing, 2007.

Kelly, Tom, and Ted Robinson. *Season of Dreams: The Minnesota Twins' Drive to the 1991 World Championship.* Osceola, Wis.: Voyageur Press, 1992.

Puckett, Kirby. *I Love This Game!: My Life and Baseball.* New York: HarperCollins Publishers, 1993.

WEB SITES

Baseball Almanac

http://www.baseball-almanac.com

BaseballLibrary.com

http://www.baseballlibrary.com

Baseball Reference

http://www.baseball-reference.com

Major League Baseball: Kirby Puckett Tribute

http://mlb.mlb.com/mlb/news/tributes/obit_kirby_puckett.jsp

Major League Baseball: The Official Site

http://mlb.mlb.com/index.jsp

National Baseball Hall of Fame and Museum

http://www.baseballhalloffame.org

The Official Site of the Minnesota Twins

http://minnesota.twins.mlb.com

WCCO: Remembering Kirby Puckett

http://wcco.com/local/local_story_067152508.html

PICTURE CREDITS

PAGE

4: AP Images
10: AP Images
17: MLB Photos via Getty Images
26: © Bettmann/CORBIS
32: AP Images
38: AP Images
45: Getty Images
49: MLB Photos via Getty Images
53: Time & Life Pictures/Getty Images
58: Getty Images
62: Time & Life Pictures/Getty Images
68: AP Images
74: AP Images
76: REUTERS/Gary Hershorn/ Landov
79: AFP/Getty Images
84: Getty Images
90: AP Images
94: Focus on Sport/ Getty Images
96: Time & Life Pictures/ Getty Images
101: AP Images
103: AP Images
107: AP Images
109: AP Images

COVER

© MLB/Getty Images

INDEX

ABOUT THE AUTHOR

RACHEL A. KOESTLER-GRACK has worked with nonfiction books as an editor and writer since 1999. During her career, she has worked extensively on historical topics, ranging from the Middle Ages to the Colonial era to the civil rights movement. In addition, she has written numerous biographies on a variety of historical and contemporary figures. She lives with her husband and daughter on a hobby farm near Glencoe, Minnesota.